EPIPHANIES, INDIVIDUATION, AND HUMAN FLOURISHING

Within this book, Gray argues that moments of profound existential importance are given to us in the presence of Art, and that such moments are important motivators in our personal, civic, and moral lives.

Using the work of Jung, Freud, Berger, and Nussbaum, this book looks to Art in its theory and practice as a driver of psychic epiphany. Examining music, environment, architecture, poetry, and painting, it traces the relationship between the ordinary and the extraordinary, showing how we can and do locate ourselves beyond our own psyches in a world of artistic endeavour. Gray concludes that Art plays a critical role in psychological practice and human flourishing on an individual and collective level.

Epiphanies, Individuation, and Human Flourishing will appeal to artists, art theorists, therapists, and analysts as a teaching tool that demonstrates the possible connections that can be made among the arts, sciences and psycho-therapeutic communities, and Nature.

Frances Gray is a philosopher with a strong interest in Jungian psychology, neuroscience, and feminism. Her work attempts to figure out the relationship between individual and collective with an emphasis of ethics and its political implications. Frances Gray is the author of the following Routledge titles: *Jung, Irigaray, Individuation: Philosophy, Analytical Psychology and the Question of the Feminine; Cartesian Philosophy and the Flesh, Reflections on Incarnation in Analytical Psychology;* and *Jung and Levinas: An Ethics of Mediation*, as well as co-editor of *Feminist Views from Somewhere.* She is an Honorary Senior Research Fellow at the University of Queensland, St Lucia, Australia.

EPIPHANIES, INDIVIDUATION, AND HUMAN FLOURISHING

Essays on Nature, Beauty, and Art

Frances Gray

Routledge
Taylor & Francis Group
LONDON AND NEW YORK

Designed cover image: *Lines of Light* by Frances Gray.

First published 2023
by Routledge
4 Park Square, Milton Park, Abingdon, Oxon OX14 4RN

and by Routledge
605 Third Avenue, New York, NY 10158

Routledge is an imprint of the Taylor & Francis Group, an informa business

British Library Cataloguing-in-Publication Data
A catalogue record for this book is available from the British Library

ISBN: 978-0-367-08544-5 (hbk)
ISBN: 978-0-367-08546-9 (pbk)
ISBN: 978-0-429-02297-5 (ebk)

DOI: 10.4324/9780429022975

Typeset in Bembo
by Newgen Publishing UK

With love and gratitude and in memory of Maria Kirsten 1966–2021

CONTENTS

LIVING BODIES AND CONSCIOUSNESS

Foundations

Our human consciousness and what 'it' is, remains a mystery that so far has eluded us, something about which we remain largely ignorant, even with recent insights. This is not, from a scientific point of view, wilful ignorance. No-one knows or has discovered the key to this mystery although there are many well thought-out guesses based on research and argument, many beliefs, many attempts to capture consciousness (Blackmore, 2005; Dennett, 1992; Metzinger, 2009; Prinz & Oxford University, 2015). So, many theories about mind, consciousness, the brain have emerged with the development of neuroscience over the past 60 years. On one account, the mind and/or consciousness can be thought of as function: consciousness is the way in which the brain functions (Levin, Fall 2018).[1] Or, perhaps the brain can be thought of as a sophisticated computational system like a Turing machine or a system of neural networks (Rescorla, 2020). Or, the mind and consciousness might emerge from the way that the brain is as either a parallel or supervenient system (Stoljar, 2020). Or, consciousness might defy the attempts of neuroscientists and philosophers and remain as a hard problem, *the hard problem or question* (Chalmers, 1995, 1996, 2018). This focus on the nature of consciousness (or even its mention) has been a fairly recent development in analytic Anglo-American philosophy. When I was a young student, it was the mind that occupied pride of place in theorising human being. That said, Indian philosophies have taken consciousness very seriously for a very long time. In Europe, phenomenology and existential philosophies, and of course, psychiatry and psychology have been the trendsetters in this domain. That said, the mechanism, if there is one and whatever it is, of awareness and self-consciousness exceeds our current knowledge or is even unknowable, something many of us are too proud to admit—that there are limits to human knowledge and even experience.

So we are in a position in which the scientific and philosophical literature on consciousness, bodies, brains, and computers (specifically artificial intelligence in the case of the latter) is vast, often contradictory and argumentative, and comes to different conclusions depending on the model developed and explored (Berent, 2020; Churchland, 2007; Churchland & Sejnowski, 2017; Colombetti, 2014; Currie & Ravenscroft, 2002; Dennett, 1992; Gallagher, 2017; Goff, 2017, 2019; Heinämaa, 2007; Koch, 2012, 2019; Metzinger, 2009; Noë, 2016; Penfield, 2015; Penrose, 2016; Prinz, 2012; Prinz & Oxford University, 2015; Rescorla, 2020; Thompson & Varela, 2001; Zahavi, 2005, 2007).[2] As I have indicated, the research is inconclusive, for while neuroscience, for instance, might show us *that* the brain is involved in various structural and functional activities of consciousness, it does not show us *how* these activities produce imagination, and insight. Nor does the research show or explain how it is that one can feel and know that one is feeling: there is little, if any, definitive explanation of the meta-activities of consciousness, the hows and whys of self-awareness. David Chalmers' 'the hard problem of consciousness' (how come I experience, how come my brain 'produces' both experience and me) remains.

Throughout this book, and given the above, I assume the following:

1. Consciousness and life belong together: consciousness is a property/quality/aspect of any living thing including the living body of a human being.
2. The brain (in humans at least) is the originary site of consciousness: no human brain no human consciousness, and no mind.
3. We do not, in spite of current research, know what consciousness is, nor do we know what life is, even if we do know some of the fundamentals of both consciousness and life (for example that consciousness involves awareness and responsiveness and that carbon is fundamental to life on Earth (as we understand 'life')).
4. We do not know how material bodies and consciousness are related to each other, even though there appears to exist some causal relationship which is bidirectional. As argued by Markus Gabriel, I am not identical with my brain: the brain is a necessary, but not sufficient condition for being me (Gabriel & Turner, 2017).
5. Drugs affect the human body, and some drugs directly affect consciousness and the mind. How does this happen?
6. Many animals experience and are, therefore, conscious.
7. Human consciousness and perhaps the consciousness of some other apes is capable of self-reflection.
8. Human consciousness is the origin of constructed culture, literary imagination, and elaborate symbolic systems
9. Human consciousness is the basis of individuation.[3]
10. Computers are inorganic machines and are not capable of consciousness: life is a necessary condition of consciousness, or in other words, to be conscious, you must be living/alive.
11. This is not to say that computers cannot imitate human consciousness; that is, they appear to be like humans say from a computational perspective (IBM's Deep Blue). Computers have been hypothesised in fiction to the extent

of *appearing to be* humans (David in the Steven Spielberg film *AI: Artificial Intelligence*; the TV series, *West World* and *Humans*). By definition, computers are not living beings: they are machines, ingenious, magnificent with great cognitive power (Damasio, 2000, 2003). Although they might engage in reasoning and can 'remember' (memory on a basic computer) and communicate (Siri) they do not breathe, give birth, eat, or drink. And we are not computers; we are organic beings.

12. Philosophers have also argued about the conceivability/inconceivability of what David Chalmers refers to as philosophical zombies, a replica of a human being but lacking in self-consciousness, or an inner life. I am agnostic about this debate amongst philosophers. That said, the debate revolves around whether or not the brain gives us the full story about consciousness and the mind. As I've indicated, I do not think it has, but I am inclined to believe that they are conceivable. See Kirk (2021) for a full discussion of zombies.
13. Finally, I would like to note that sometimes I shall refer to consciousness, sometimes to mind or self or soul. These terms are all related to each other, with consciousness at their centre. Body and soul we are, each one of us. In a footnote in Chapter 1 of *The Therapy of Desire*, Martha Nussbaum remarks on her use of 'soul':

> The word "soul," here and elsewhere, simply translates Greek psuchē, and, like that term, does not imply any particular metaphysical theory of the personality. It stands, simply, for all the life-activities of the creature; in the case of Hellenistic contrasts between body and psuchē, it is especially important to insist that no denial of physicalism need be involved, since both Epicureans and Stoics are physicalists. The contrast is simply between the material constituents of the organism and its life-activities, its states of awareness, and so forth.
>
> *Nussbaum, 2013: 13*

I follow suit, noting that I have questions rather than theories about the metaphysical nature of personality.

I do not argue for any of these assumptions or points of view. In my opinion, there is more missing than there is found and secured in scientific research and phenomenological studies of human consciousness. So in what follows, there will be reference to some of these views, and, hopefully, why I accept judiciously, and perhaps tentatively, the above.

My own understanding of consciousness begins with the basic idea that consciousness or awareness is responsiveness. Responsiveness to what? Consider this

> Husserl takes up again the *Critique of Judgement* when he talks about a teleology of consciousness. It is not a matter of duplicating human consciousness with some absolute thought which, from outside, is imagined as assigning to it its aims. **It is a question of recognising consciousness itself as a**

> **project of the world, meant for a world which it neither embraces nor possesses, but towards which it is perpetually directed – and the world as this pre-objective individual whose imperious unity decrees what knowledge shall take as its goal.**
>
> *Merleau-Ponty, 1995: xvii–xviii, my emphasis*

Merleau-Ponty's remark that consciousness is a project of the world suggests that it broadly inhabits the world, for he seems to be attributing to consciousness an existence deeply embedded in the structure of the world. The world is *directed* through its own striving, as Baruch de Spinoza would have it, always towards something which is in its own purview. The world, of which humans are part, is the home of consciousness, and in which humans live but which is not the product of human existence. The world is a conscious world which gives birth to humans who enjoy the fruits of awareness and responsiveness. The idea that consciousness is a project of the world foreshadows the recent renaissance of panpsychism as a possible way of understanding consciousness. David Chalmers signalled this possibility and Christof Koch has taken it up in *The Feeling of Life Itself.*

Hence, 'consciousness' here is not to be understood as a property/feature/quality/of human beings alone. Rather, 'consciousness' permeates the world: in other words, 'consciousness' is found as part of this world in its evolution. In this conception of consciousness, if some living thing is responsive, it is conscious. Thus if we observe a sunflower and we see how it moves with the sun, how it responds, how it strives in its own being, to exist, we are observing a form of primitive consciousness. This is cellular awareness in a sunflower.[4] Cellular awareness, responsiveness is intrinsic to all consciousness.

But, and this is a big 'but', the awareness in terms of responsiveness and awareness that is present in plants is qualitatively unlike that in human beings. From both an evolutionary and a bio-structural perspective, the sophistication of human awareness/responsiveness/consciousness is way more complex, more intricate. We might think of this as a kind of hierarchy of sophistication in which smaller and simpler organisms are conscious, but less so, than those that are bigger and more complex. The human brain has developed from a fight/flight organ whose basic function is preservation of life, based upon feeling and emotion, into the simple core consciousness and the multifaceted extended consciousness about which Antonio Damasio writes (Damasio, 2000: 16).

Although it is common practice amongst researchers in this area, I shall not talk of consciousness in terms of representation. I do not believe that I represent myself to myself nor do I represent the world to myself. I experience and engage with myself and the world. In my view 'represent' as a way of speaking about consciousness is ill-chosen and reflects underlying misguided ontological assumptions. Antonio Damasio, for example, slips into its use early in *The Feeling of What Happens* (Damasio, 2000: 22). I say 'slips into its use' while acknowledging that he does discuss its meaning in the Appendix to *The Feeling of What Happens.* He says that it is 'a problematic but virtually inevitable term in discussions of this sort' followed by

> My mental image of a particular face is a representation, and so are the neural patterns that arise during the perceptual-motor processing of that face, in a variety of visual, somatosensory, and motor regions of the brain. This use of *representation* (his italics) is conventional and transparent. It simply means "pattern that is consistently related to something," whether with respect to mental image or to a coherent set of neural activities within a specific brain region.
>
> *Damasio, 2000: 11, 320*

Damasio goes on to explain that even if you and I form comparable images of an object, it is because of the way in which our brains work, rather than mirror-like fidelity to the outside world because we have no way of knowing whether or not the image we form is an exact copy of that object, even though an 'external reality' might 'prompt' its creation. He argues for an interactionist view of the images we form in our minds. This interaction between objects and the brain's neural activities is what creates those images of objects (Damasio, 2000: 320–321). I suspect Damasio's use echoes a 'naturalised' Kantian ontology. Immanuel Kant also had argued representations and the faculty of representation (*Vorstellungen*) (Kant, 1933: 34, 75, 77 passim) related to his metaphysical distinction between appearances and things-as-they-are. The point that Kant argues is that we humans do not have an immediate and direct relationship with an external world, but that we represent it to ourselves the world through appearances for which our minds and cognition are responsible.[5]

It is clear that images and representations are closely linked. However, note that Damasio's rendering of 'representation' is visually oriented, even though his discussion of 'image' invokes sound (Damasio, 2000: 318). This seems to be in keeping with other work on the relationship between consciousness and the external world and our experience of it in which work on consciousness and cognition focuses (no pun intended) on vision, together with colour perception (Varela et al., 2016: 147 ff). Even if it can be shown that many different factors affect colour perception it does not follow that we are engaged in representation. What we touch and are touched by, as I shall argue shortly, cuts across the idea of representation as outlined here.

In my view, we also have no way of knowing that images we form are *not* exact copies, in some respects, of an object. This does not mean, though, that the mind is always or is never a mirror image of the world we live in. We do not experience the world in micro-detail. A snake about to strike me is a snake about to strike me, just as lightning is lightning and death is death. From a phenomenological perspective, the world is as it is, unless we have clear reason to believe that is not the case. The natural attitude, which can be thought of in terms of the world's being what we experience it to be, grounds our very understanding of ourselves and the world. Of course we do make judgements, we can be right or wrong and we can invoke the *epoché* as Edmund Husserl argued, to get at the essence of things. But on an everyday basis, we are not mistaken for most of the time. We might hypothesise and discover the subatomic world, but we cannot and do not experience that world from the inside as it were. And we use the furniture of this world as we understand and experience it, to make these hypotheses and discoveries (electron microscopes, Large Hadron Collider). We shall come to this point again, in the next chapter. For now, I maintain that our experience of the world gives us the best possible idea of ourselves and our environment, importantly from the inside, and from a manufactured 'outside' in which others like-us become objects-to-us.

Pierre Hadot distinguishes between the world of science and the world of everyday perception. He regards the world of science as unrepresentable, constructed by scientists. He says:

> The world of science does indeed, by means of its multiple technical applications, radically transform some aspects of our daily life. Yet it is essential to realise that our way of perceiving the world in everyday life is not radically affected by scientific conceptions. For all of us – even the astronomer, when he goes home at night – the sun rises and sets, and the earth is immobile.
>
> *Hadot, 2011*

As we shall see, this does not mean that we are limited by our everyday perceptions/ conceptions of the world. Epiphany, transformation are always possible. That is perhaps one of the great gifts diversely offered to us by Sigmund Freud, Carl Jung, and their teachers and peers. What that means is that consciousness (and, indeed, unconsciousness as a mode of existential experience) is central to all of this. Without responsiveness, without awareness and its development, we do not exist as self-reflexive creatures. Merleau-Ponty's idea that consciousness is a project of the world is spot-on, but the origin of consciousness and the world, how they come to be in the first place, is unknown and probably unknowable. What we do know, now, however, is that human beings are not the only living beings who are conscious. Christof Koch's discussion of his relationship with his dog is a beautiful and illuminating illustration of this (Koch, 2019).

At its basis, the idea that we *represent* the world to ourselves arises because of our failure to acknowledge the interconnectedness of humans and Nature, even with say, a Buddhist mindfulness orientation (Thompson, 2010; Varela et al., 2016). So by way of contrast, I want to note that for some Buddhists, consciousness and suffering are intertwined. On the whole, Buddhists attempt to explain the cause of suffering and argue that it is because we have the mistaken notion of a self, yes, connected to consciousness, that we suffer. It is important for them, therefore, to show that the cause actually does not exist: if there is no self, there will be no suffering. But this is something that we have to learn by un-learning what might be thought of as our ontological commitment to self. In this view, one realises that one experiences nothing but experience(s): consciousness if 'emptied' of self. There is no self that experiences, there is simply conscious awareness, and constant change. In effect, this is to attribute moral and psychological dispositions to an error of judgement, and that error is that we are ignorant in believing in an ontologically grounded reality. Perhaps what is needed is an idea of self that does not rely on the idea of an unchanging substance, but, instead, incorporates change and fluidity. This would agree with the changeableness we all experience in our lives. However, it would not address the central role of conscious awareness and memory with which most of us identify.

Khenpo Tsultrim Gyamtso Rinpoche remarks that

> Our instinctive, emotional attachment or clinging to a vague notion of self is the source of all our suffering. From the idea of 'self' comes that of 'other'. It is from the interaction of 'self and 'other' that desire, hatred and delusion arise. There are many kinds of desire including greed, envy and miserliness. Hatred can take the form of jealousy, anger and resentment. Delusion includes mental dullness, stupidity and confusion. From these unhealthy mental states arise actions motivated by them, and their results. The results take the form of all kinds of sufferings, which one cannot escape as long as one identifies with the 'self' who is suffering.
>
> *Gyamtso, 1986/1988/1994: 33*

In my view, the idea of self does not precede the idea of other, if that is what is meant by 'from the idea of 'self' comes that of 'other'. The connection is there, but *reversed* and is a given of phenomenology as we have just seen in Merleau-Ponty. The interaction of self and other might be a cause of suffering, but that it is pathological is not a given as Gyamtso's claim suggests. Self and other interact in multiple ways, all of which do not result in suffering. Certainly if we grasp at things or experiences or other persons, and are unsatisfied or disappointed in our efforts, suffering will ensue. And cognition plays an important role in this, for knowledge and ignorance, important cognitive elements are at the forefront to some kinds of conscious awareness. And learning to deal with all of this helps with our capacity to individuate, to become a self-reflecting conscious presence in the world.

The Enactivist Approach

Enactivism (neuroscience, philosophy, and psychology) implicitly acknowledges our complete immersion in the worlds in which we find ourselves. Enactivism has been developed and further explored by Thompson (2010, 2011), Shaun Gallagher (2017) and Giovanna Colombetti (2014) amongst others. They take seriously phenomenological insights arising from Franz Brentano, Edmund Husserl, Martin Heidegger, and Maurice Merleau-Ponty. In earlier work, I have referred to Brentano's intentionality thesis (Gray, 2012, 2016). My emphasis there has been, primarily, on tracing possible influences that Brentano might have had on C. G. Jung. Mostly, my interest has been in the representational aspects of intentionality—that is to say the notion of there being an object of mental events and whether or not such objects need be conscious, a problem with which Brentano concerns himself (Brentano et al., 1995 II: Inner Consciousness). Indeed by far, the bulk of scholarship on Brentano's idea and the idea of intentionality subsequently has revolved around the status of mental objects, and it appears that such debates and controversies also have some bearing on the relationship between psychoanalysis and phenomenology (Jacob, 2019; Siewert, 2017).

As Varela, Thompson and Rosch point out, representation has been a key theme in cognitive science and computer modelling. But enactivist theorists rethink the notion of intentionality away from representation and towards the mutuality, even the reciprocity, of activity, of being in the world in the mode of Merleau-Ponty. For them, cognition is 'always about or directed toward something that is missing', a next step or a situation in the world (Varela et al., 1991: 205). And Varela, Thompson, and Rosch explore cognition through cognitive science and its origins, and phenomenology. They introduce the Buddhist practice of mindfulness as a possible avenue for bringing together the whole of human experience in a way that is understandable from scientific, phenomenological and personal, experiential perspectives.[6]

Specifically, the Buddhism to which they refer is Tibetan in the tradition of Mahayana, the Buddhism of Gyamtso. They argue, using the Buddhist Aggregates (forms; feelings/sensations; perceptions (discernments)/impulses; dispositional formations; consciousness), that all 'five together constitute the psychophysical complex that makes up a person and that makes up each moment of experience' (Varela et al., 2016: 64). They imagine what it would be to be in pursuit of the 'real self' which each of us takes ourselves to be. They conclude that the real self is not in any one of the aggregates, nor is it in the sum of the aggregates, that 'no such real self is given to us in our experience' (Varela et al., 2016: 69). After exploring and rejecting alternatives from the Western tradition (Descartes' *res cogitans* and Kant's transcendental ego) they conclude that the search for a real, substantial self will always be frustrated. From the perspective of the present moment, we cannot discover a self that persists in our experience.

The trio identifies a circularity in thinking about cognition: 'that our cognition emerges from the background of a world that extends beyond us but that cannot be found apart from our embodiment'. In their research, they argue that there is no abiding self, no foundation, no objective ground that can be identified as an unchanging, foundational self, always present in experience. The self is an illusion:

> (w)hen we tried to find the objective ground that we thought must still be present, we found a world enacted by our history of structural coupling … organism and environment fold into one another in the fundamental circularity that is life itself.
>
> *Varela et al., 1991: 217*

How do they get to this position? In part, they accept the Buddhist idea of no-self.

In Buddhist traditions, meditation, sometimes characterised as mindfulness (becoming aware that one's mental life is composed of a succession of present moments that slip away and can never be held) and *Zazen* bring about the realisation that change means that there is no substantial self. Buddhists argue either that there is no substantial self or that they are agnostic about the self.[7] It is the practice of meditation that brings one to this conclusion. With practice, fully engaged meditation is a non-narrative experience in which focus on the breath or bodily sensations becomes a conscious, sensuous experience, unfettered by any assumptions or ontological commitments. The silence and peacefulness that ensue bring relief from suffering. In my view, the *success* of this practice is a cognitive insight: you have to be able to *do* it though. *Doing* it, though, does not provide the grounds for the ontological assumptions that Buddhists have developed out of meditation. Indeed, the focus on one's own consciousness foregoes the possibility of taking seriously the claims of phenomenology, and of enactivism, and Buddhism. Hence I wonder about the conclusion, an ontological claim, that the meditator reaches—that there is no substantial self. That is, a basis of their claim, that experience of the ever-changing mind/consciousness does not entail the conclusion that there is no self, so something more is needed.

So although I have just said that mindfulness is unfettered by any assumptions or ontological commitments, which amounts to a commitment to groundlessness, viz. that everything is empty and constantly changing, there seems to me to be an enthymeme operating here, that there is a 'my' to the awareness and experience I take to be mine. Meditation on the succession of present moments, it is held, shows that self is not substantial. However, the discovery of groundlessness or no-mind is based on the practice of conscious, watchful awareness on the part of the meditator. I wonder then, about the conception of no-self which is the result of the practice: who or what is experiencing, and who or what is aware? I might say, for instance, 'So what? I know I am constantly changing, but it is the I (me) that knows this that is in question, not what I know to be the case in my changing world, i.e. that my self changes. What is the "I" that cognizes?'

Varela, Thompson, and Rosch imagine that a reader might pose a question related to my concerns:

> How is it, if we have no self, that there is a coherence in our lives? How is it, if we have no self that, that we continue to think, feel, and act as though we had a self –endlessly seeking to enhance and defend the non-definable, non-experienced self?
>
> *Varela et al., 2016: 110*

They appeal to the Buddhist understanding of *karma* which they characterise as an 'historical formation of various patterns and trends in our lives' and assert that it is 'this accumulation that gives continuity to the sense of ego-self, so evident in everyday, unreflective life' (Varela et al., 2016: 116). In other words, they conclude that *karma* provides an answer. There is a couple of problems with this.

Firstly, what does it mean to say that the self is non-definable and non-experienced. Certainly, the self, as a substantial entity, might not be definable, and non-experienced? But perhaps the self is simply the experience, the referential, reflexive experience that takes one back to one's consciousness in memory and reflection? And that does not have to be definable, and will it always be given in experience because that is the nature of consciousness? There needs to be an argument that shows the necessity of conceiving of the self as a persistent, unchanging, substance. That is not provided, merely assumed. And this brings me to my next worry about this solution. As I see it, the language of *having* serves only to exacerbate the problem because it raises this question: what is it that *has* a self? If there *is* nothing that *has*, then there is no having in the first place. This language surely underscores the whole question of mind and consciousness: just what exactly are they? Speaking of the Buddha or the wisdom mind further highlights the quandary—in the process of realising groundlessness or emptiness, it seems clear that something does the realising. Some 'thing' or phenomenon is enlightened or at least there is an enlightenment experience, but it makes sense that if there is an experience, then there must be an experiencer *if there is awareness*. And, yes, there is awareness! I am reminded here of Nietzsche's and Russell's claims that there does not have to be an experiencer for there to be an experience. One is pressed to ask can there be thinking without a thinker? Perhaps Descartes assumed that there needs to be a thinker, his *I*, but how does one prove that one is an *I*? And surely if there is *awareness of experience* (thinking, believing, opining, and experiencing itself), it is clear that something is aware: there *is* a subject of awareness, and this is perhaps the reflexive understanding of 'self'.

I am also puzzled about the ready acceptance of the inference made to the ontological stance that everything has the same groundless status as self is problematic. One realises in experiencing the *skandhas* or the Five Aggregates, in which one cannot locate a self, either individually or as a whole that something else might be going on. And we do not have to take the Buddhist line on this. Aristotle, for example, notes that

> (i)n the case of all things which have several parts and in which the totality is not, as it were, a mere heap, but the whole is something besides the parts, there is a cause; for even in bodies contact is the cause of unity in some cases, and in others viscosity or some other such quality.
>
> *Aristotle & McKeon, 1941: 1045a 8–12*

If we think of the self as having several 'parts' (constituents, aspects) and the self as a totality, which is not a mere heap, but something besides the parts (a reflexive awareness for example) which is not merely the 'circular structure of habitual patterns' and that the whole (the parts and the something besides) has a cause, then we might be able to come up with a working notion of self that does not depend on the notion of self as persistent, unchanging substance. We might, for example, argue that self is indeed caused by the world in which we live, together with the (reflexive) workings of consciousness, itself a property of the world, in this case, of human beings in the world; and human beings *are* bodies. Thus consciousness is a property of bodies and self is its reflexive awareness. This is a view in which the causal nexus is viewed as the phenomenological coexistence of consciousness and other, in which 'I' and 'self' are experiential 'parts'. And it is paradoxical, yes.

Hence we could discern here, a primitive notion of the self as both an effect of cause(s) and a constituted entity beyond what constitutes it (that's the paradox). We acknowledge the phenomenological nature of self and other, and at the same time preserve the ontological integrity of other. There is a strong, ontological sense in which the world, in other words, *is* (not can be) separate from phenomenological consciousness (the world pre-exists any consciousness as it will post-exist it), while at the same time, self is both epistemologically and phenomenologically dependent. This is the sense in which the world and consciousness are intertwined. One's being as a self is phenomenological being. This enlightened view is an aspect of individuation. I shall have more to say about this in the following chapters. We can retain the idea that self is enacted, but that enactment is phenomenological, and self requires the ontological, participatory, integrity of the world.

Lastly, I maintain that there are two moments of consciousness: pre-narrative and narrative consciousness, about which I also shall have more to say in later chapters. A basic division, then, exists between unconscious, primitive experience and self-conscious, aware, experience. The importance of these assumptions about bodies and consciousness will become clear as I discuss what I think of as psychological epiphany, Nature, Beauty, and Art and their dependence on the idea of change. The link to individuation, to the deep awareness of self as reflective consciousness, vital and ever changing but nonetheless persistently aware, will become clear, I hope.

Notes

1

> Functionalism is the doctrine that what makes something a thought, desire, pain (or any other type of mental state) depends not on its internal constitution, but solely on its function, or the role it plays, in the cognitive system of which it is a part. More precisely, functionalist theories take the identity of a mental state to be determined by its causal relations to sensory stimulations, other mental states, and behavior.
>
> *Levin, 2018*

2 This is a small sample of what is available in the research.
3 When I use the term 'individuation' I am using it in a Jungian sense as I have in my previous books.
4 See Atamian et al. (2016).
5 See Kant (1998: passim) and Brook and Wuerth (2020). Note that there is much written on this topic.
6 A new edition of which was published in 2017 with a Foreword by Jon Kabat-Zinn, a master of mindfulness teaching. Francisco Varela died in 2001; the new Introductions are by the surviving co-authors.
7 See, for example, *Progressive Stages of Meditation on Emptiness* in which Rinpoche argues that 'the self is simply a vague and convenient concept that we project now here and now there on to a stream of experiences, and is nothing in or of itself' (Gyamtso, 1986/1988/1994: 31).

INTRODUCTION

> Herein lay the spring of the mechanical art and mystery of educating the reason without stooping to the cultivation of the sentiments and affections. Never wonder. By means of addition, subtraction, multiplication, and division, settle everything somehow, and never wonder.
>
> *Charles Dickens* Hard Times *69*[1]

In many ways, this book is a footnote to my previous books. It returns to narrative, to subjectivity, to Jung and philosophy. But it alludes to Jungian themes, rather than critically examining them. Fundamentally, epiphanic moments are about individuation. I hope that this becomes clear as the book develops. The context of this whole project is in the following:

> Suddenly the piercing cry of a night heron awakened me as if from a dream. All the confusion, all the agony that had obsessed me disappeared with the morning mist. Something I call 'true nature' was revealed. I had been transformed body and soul ... The peaceful beauty of the world became vividly apparent to me. I was overcome with emotion and reduced to trembling ... I became as light as the wings of a dragonfly, and felt as if I were flying as high as the mountain peaks.
>
> *Fukuoka, 2021: 2*

I hope this book brings you to Nature, Beauty, and Art through phenomenology,[2] and psychology and then on to Ethics and the Moral Life as practice and transformation.

In *Cartesian Philosophy and the Flesh*, I worked with Pierre Hadot's idea that philosophy is practice. Hadot developed his thesis from his intensive study of ancient

DOI: 10.4324/9780429022975-1

philosophy in which he argued that one did not simply *read* philosophy, but one *lived* philosophy. For Marcus Aurelius, morality was the most important facet of philosophy for, as Marcus argued, one's morality is the only thing over which one has control. The past has happened, the future is yet to happen. Marcus is, in my view, quite right. But Marcus promotes the idea of repelling the human body in order to achieve detachment and thus to remain indifferent to the world.

The essays in this book highlight the fact that human beings are, ontologically, conscious and self-conscious animals in Nature, and that much, indeed most of the whole world, built and Natural, are ontologically independent of our wills, even when we are responsible for creating non-Natural objects. *ontos*, Being,[3] is not dependent on human consciousness but phenomenology is. Phenomenology is not ontology.[4] We are born *into* pre-existing Nature and social worlds which cease to exist for us when we die (since we cease to exist). But Nature and those worlds persist beyond and above and behind our individual and collective existences. Any living thing comes into, and goes out, of existence. That is the cycle of Nature, the cycle of being. We live in a Natural world, a world of the elements on which we are dependent. Using the materials of the Natural world, we make other worlds on which we also might become dependent. We are not 'outside' worlds we believe we create, phenomenologically speaking: indeed we are agents who use the materials of the world without which we cannot create. We are never, *phenomenologically speaking*, 'outside' even when our consciousnesses suggest that we can be and are. Yet we are unlike the rocks and water and clouds and air: we are conscious and we *experience* both our Natural and built environments and their products. We can symbolise those worlds in language and the arts, and in the sciences. Nevertheless, we remain ignorant.[5] Greek and Indian metaphysicians saw ignorance as a flaw in our natures, especially wilful ignorance. Wilful ignorance grounds our being in many ways, and is, as the Buddhists say, the cause of suffering; and it also attests to our mental laziness. It's easier to make things up, develop a narrative, than to go to the bother of finding things out through research and simply being openly observant. That is not to say that all narrative is fictional, or that things we make up are always wrong. We can develop hypotheses and test them. They might be on the mark and they might not be.

I've addressed the idea of making things up in my discussion of narrative in *Jung and Levinas* (Gray, 2016) and my use of the term 'narrative' is an extension of those ideas. There, I argued for the importance of narrative as a constituent of self-making, and I do not wander too much from that view. You will see that narrative, and its contrary, non-narrative, play an important role throughout this book.

Alexander Nehamas opens his 2001 Tanner Lectures at Yale University with this question, 'What happens to us when something—something we see for the first time or have perhaps known for long—reveals its beauty to us, and, suddenly transfigured, takes our breath away and makes time stand still?' (Nehamas, 2001). It could be that Nehamas is asking a question about the very same moments of which I speak. Yet his response deals directly with the philosophical canon, which, on the whole, has side-stepped what I call non-narrative existential moments with the possible exception of philosophical literature dealing with religious experience.[6] To pre-empt an answer: what happens to us is that we strike out, that is to say, begin, or continue, on the path to individuation.

Nehamas' response to his question does not go there, but takes us across philosophy's historical terrain beginning with Plato and then, in contrast, moving to Schopenhauer. He contrasts Plato's love of the beautiful body with Schopenhauer's identification of Beauty as an abstract concept, away from emotion and desire, with works of Art.

> When Plato thinks of beauty, he first thinks of beautiful people – most often, beautiful boys. Paederastic desire is the initial step toward the highest beauties he values; but these – the beauty of souls, of laws and ways of life, of learning – however abstract, persist in provoking passion, longing … Modeled on the human form and its power, beauty is for Plato inseparable from yearning and desire …
>
> The beauty of the human form, to the extent that it is an object of passion, is irrelevant to Schopenhauer … Desire, yearning, and passion are just what Schopenhauer wants to escape from; beauty, as he conceives it, is the surest means of liberating us from the shackles of the will, which, since it "springs from lack, from deficiency and thus from suffering," can never be content and is the source of constant misery. All satisfaction is ephemeral.
>
> *Nehamas, 2001: 190*

Both Plato and Schopenhauer contextualise Beauty within a temporal frame. Plato's Socrates remarks that the newly initiated 'who has had a full sight of the celestial vision, when he beholds a god-like face or a physical form which truly reflects ideal beauty, first of all shivers and experiences something of the dread which the vision itself inspire; next he gazes upon it and worships it as if it were a god' is indeed courting divine love (Plato, 1973: § 251). And Schopenhauer argues that denunciation of (the power of) the will is necessary

> Therefore, so long as our consciousness is filled by our will, so long as we are given up to the throng of desires with their constant hopes and fears, so long as we are the subject of willing, we can never have lasting happiness nor peace. It is essentially all the same whether we pursue or flee, fear injury or seek enjoyment; the care for the constant demands of the will, in whatever form it may be, continually occupies and sways the consciousness; but without peace no true wellbeing is possible … But when some external cause or inward disposition lifts us suddenly out of the endless stream of willing, delivers knowledge from the slavery of the will, the attention is no longer directed to the motives of willing, but comprehends things free from their relation to the will, and thus observes them without personal interest, without subjectivity, purely objectively, gives itself entirely up to them so far as they are ideas, but not in so far as they are motives.
>
> *Schopenhauer, 2012: § 38*

The experiences about which I am writing belong more with Schopenhauer and the abandonment of the will than they do with Mihaly Csikszentmihalyi and, possibly, with Plato. The lengthy response which Nehamas gives to the question he raises argues for a connection between Beauty and Art. But he rejects the idea that all Art is beautiful and weaves, instead, a story that tells us that Beauty is more like love. 'For love, as Plato saw, is beauty's attendant and constant companion. To love someone just is to find them beautiful …'. Part of his conclusion is that Beauty provokes desire, and contra Schopenhauer is the object of love (Nehamas, 2001: 204, 206).

When we are moved by something that is beautiful, we may be stirred in the very same way in which we are stirred by love of another. Nehamas does not deal with the distinction that Schopenhauer makes between the will and knowledge. It seems to me that Nehamas overlooks the psychological insight had by Schopenhauer—that the subjective element is at play in the appreciation of Beauty in the moment of.... wonder? transport? delight? For Schopenhauer, our wills are side-lined as we enter a world of perfect knowing. This is what he says:

> In all these reflections it has been my object to bring out clearly the nature and the scope of the subjective element in aesthetic pleasure; the deliverance of knowledge from the service of the will, the forgetting of self as an individual, and the raising of the consciousness to the pure will-less, timeless, subject of knowledge, independent of all relations. With this subjective side of aesthetic contemplation, there must always appear as its necessary correlative the objective side, the intuitive comprehension of the Platonic Idea.
>
> *Schopenhauer, 1844: § 38*

Now I do not know if we do intuitively comprehend the Platonic Idea (of Beauty); an intelligible Form is difficult to conceive even if one does know what perfection is, intuitively or by any other means. Perhaps perfection is either a human fabrication or beyond human imagination and intellectual skill? What I do realise, though, is that Schopenhauer's insight pinpoints the unintentional nature of non-narrative existential moments. As we shall see shortly, 'the deliverance of knowledge from the service of the will, the forgetting of self as an individual, and the raising of the consciousness to the pure will-less, timeless, subject of knowledge' are some of the features of non-narrative existential moments. That said, Nehamas can help us to understand the nature of the existential moment when it is narrativised, in the promise of the extension of Beauty beyond Art. But I do believe that Schopenhauer is correct in his invocation of an objective correlate to a subjective experience. We do not invent the worlds in which we live; to reiterate, ontologically speaking, the world as a whole, is not a product of human consciousness. In this sense, it is important to acknowledge the apartness of the world, above all, the apartness of Nature from which we seem to have separated ourselves as if Nature and ourselves were not of the same *ontos*. Climate change and environmental damage are the witnesses of this. How we conceive of that objective correlate in a time when the subject/object distinction has come under fire, is a quandary. The world is *apart* from us, however, we are not separate from the world, indeed a part of the world, both ontologically in our physical being, and phenomenologically. Phenomenologically, we suffer the *illusion of separateness*. The distinction I am making here does not entail dualism, but yes, it is a dichotomy. Ontologically, however, Natures privileged over human consciousness with consciousness's phenomenological apprehension of the world.

I leave this stage setting using Plato, Schopenhauer, and Nehamas and begin to explore non-narrative existential moments and the epiphanic. These moments are a result of suspension of our propensity to tell ourselves a story, to narrate our lives, and give way to transformative, enlightened and enriching ways of being in the world. I hope to elucidate these terms more fully as we look at examples throughout the book, and as I discuss their importance to analytical psychology.

So this is the foundation of my thinking: that we are in and of Nature, and that phenomenology proceeds from ontology. Beauty (the beautiful) and Art, I argue, have their origin in Nature, even when social belief and practice as expounded or assumed in phenomenology propose that they are a result of practice and fashion. One of the consequences of this view is that we are inescapably Natural no matter what we do, or how we think of ourselves. The problem is that this is not a view shared by, or is obvious to, many people. Some philosophers, though, take the problem to heart. Dan Zahavi cites Edmund Husserl, Maurice Merleau-Ponty, and Francisco Varela and colleagues (Eleanor Rosch and Evan Thompson) who have tackled a related approach, that of naturalising phenomenology (Zahavi, 2016).

Our immersion in the modern Western world, it might be argued, precipitates against understanding Nature as the ground, the cause, of all that there is for us. We implant artificial devices and limbs and joints into human bodies, we make artificial intelligences that can perform or even out-perform human capabilities. We seem to leave Nature behind, even improve upon or transcend, our Natural bodies/minds. That we can do these things serves, I believe, to obscure our being in and of Nature, but not only that, serves to obscure our dependence on the Natural world. They also overlook the effect that our efforts to improve or overcome our Natural being has lead to environmental degradation and destruction, the loss of habitat, and extinction, for many non-human creatures; and also the devastating change in climate that affects everything on this beautiful Earth. In short, we are in and of Nature, and we depend, inextricably, on Nature; and yet we are rampaging destroyers of our home, Nature.

We are, then in, of, and transformed by, Nature: by the ecosphere in which we live, by the ecological environment. And as creative beings, we have come up with ways in which we are transformers of Nature. These two aspects of transformation—patient or acted upon, and agent—together with the fact that we can represent ourselves as beyond and apart from Nature suggest an even greater, two-headed dilemma, a practical and theoretical problem: denial of our animality, of our Natural being on the one hand, and a supremacist, androcentric 'we are above Nature' attitude, on the other.

We move earth, we collect water, we mix water and earth, we use fire to heat and enact long-lasting changes to the newly modelled earth. And we breathe, and move. We take earth and extract its colours and make shapes with our hands on surfaces that might bear our imprints for thousands of years. Immediately we are in a realm that invokes the stuff of the world—water, earth, fire, our hands. Some of this is the stuff from which we are born and to which we give birth, and to which we return. In *doing* these activities, we are creative actors as we change and respond to the changes that we make. We *do* these things not only to enhance our worlds aesthetically, but also to make things to use. Utility is one of the drivers of human activity. And we change ourselves, creatively, and the stuff of the Natural world in pursuit of Beauty and utility and profit. We are animals in Nature who have learned to transform the world around us in practical and in pleasing, symbolic, ways.[7] We bring ourselves, creatively, as makers, to using the earth and its riches. Some of us as makers excel: we seem to be able to do things with raw materials that other humans cannot do. We can draw or use colour or mould or chip away or design or build in ways that seem remarkable. That we change the world for profit adds to an already problematic notions of representation, acted upon, and agent for change.

Eureka, Peak, Optimal, Epiphany.... Those Moments

Research has shown that creativity, imagination, inspiration, and sudden insight have something to do with brain activity as well as social context. Research has also shown that diverse activities from running to listening to music, painting a picture to attending a gym or yoga class, to dancing and weight training, can produce psychological modifications that are triggered by an influx to the brain, of various hormones which consequently alter the psyche, by changing perception of one's own state and social apprehension. In these activities one can experience a feeling of oneness with our environment which suggests the collapsing of boundaries and a re-affirmation of our union with the world in which we are living and participating in this moment. Kelly McGonagal's recent work highlights much of this (McGonagal, 2020). What we experience in and through movement as transformative, marks our psyches and perhaps originates in our brains. In the former case, when an unexpected but longed for insight occurs, fMRI and EEG show neural activity in the brain that appear to correspond with reports of experiences had by research subjects (Kounios & Beeman, 2015: 63–71).

The everyday transformation that takes place as we put on our running shoes or don our swimmers, the excited anticipation we feel as we imagine the activity we are about to engage in is, on some occasions, 'peak' or optimal or even a eureka moment. We feel whole, a oneness with where we are and what we are doing. We can feel incredibly well-disposed to our fellow creatures and enraptured by our surroundings. Our eureka moments, should we have them, also produce a feeling of excitement and well-being, and perhaps relief. Some of these moments are creative moments for what they produce or engender (Demarin & Derke, 2020). All of these moments produce a positive, and transformative alteration in consciousness which might be temporary. In spite of their temporary nature, some of the moments are life altering in the long term.

McGonagal's work sits within a field of scholarship and research populated by figures such as Abraham Maslow, Mihaly Csikszentmihalyi, John Kounios, and Mark Beeman, and others who have explored insight, creativity, and psychological transformation. It was Abraham Maslow, who, from the late 1940s, began to talk about what he called peak experiences, that is to say experiences that took the subject into a different and uplifting plane. He explored peak experiences in relation to what it means to be a self-actualising person, that is to say a person who has 'attained a high level of maturation, health, and self-fulfilment'. He argues that the

> great lesson from the true mystics, from the Zen monks, and now also from the–Humanistic and transpersonal psychologists–that the sacred is in the ordinary, that it is to be found in one's daily life, in one's neighbours, friends, and family, in one's backyard, and that travel may be a flight from confronting the sacred can be easily lost. To be looking elsewhere for miracles is to me a sure sign of ignorance that everything is miraculous.
>
> *Maslow, 2012*

Following Maslow, Mihaly Csikszentmihalyi explored what he terms 'optimal experience' or 'flow'. Csikszentmihalyi engaged in research that attended to 'what people do, feel, and think during their daily lives' (Csikszentmihalyi, 2014: 21) and from this research, he developed a

> theory of optimal experience based on the concept of flow – the state in which people are so involved in what an activity that nothing else seems to matter; the experience itself is so enjoyable that people will do it even at great cost, for the sheer sake of doing it.
>
> *Csikszentmihalyi, 2009: 4*

Csikszentmihalyi believed that the results of his research can be used to help overcome disillusion, discontent, and to achieve autonomy. He proposed that we have to learn to 'provide rewards' for ourselves and to 'develop the ability to find enjoyment and purpose regardless of external circumstances' (Csikszentmihalyi, 2009: 16). He is probably right.

His research involved self-reporting as well as the articulation of goals (Csikszentmihalyi, 2014: 21–52).[8] In addition to being able to articulate goals, he argued, one needs to be aware of rules. His examples of flow activities '(p)lay, art, pageantry, ritual and sports' aimed to provide enjoyable experiences which gave 'a sense of discovery, a creative feeling of transporting the person into a new reality … In short, it transformed the self by making it more complex' (Csikszentmihalyi, 2009: 72, 74). He claimed that (a) when the activity one engages in contains a clear set of goals; that there is (b) a balance between perceived challenges and perceived skills; and that (c) flow is dependent on the presence of clear and immediate feedback and argued that they 'are all necessary features of activities that promote the intrinsically rewarding experiential involvement that characterizes flow' (Csikszentmihalyi, 2014:232). From Csikszentmihalyi's research and the subsequent theory he developed, it becomes clear that people are transformed by focus, concentration, and controlling the quality and direction of their experience (Csikszentmihalyi, 2009: 16; ff).

In my view, the ideas of peak, eureka, and optimal experience, spontaneous or not, and which can include awe, wonder, enlightenment, and the numinous, belong to the same family of *transformative phenomenological* experiences. I think of what all of this research is talking about, as *phenomenological*, since the research attends to the feelings a subject has when they experience; subjects talk about what they feel like as subjects; and what the object of their engagement feels like. This latter is a difficult distinction to make as Dan Zahavi argues. He claims that there are two aspects to the question of 'what it is like': 'what is the object like for the subject' (the I or the you) and 'what the experience of the object is like for the subject'. He argues that although we can make a conceptual distinction between these two, 'they cannot be separated'. Zahavi asks, 'When I touch the cold surface of the refrigerator, is the sensation of coldness that I feel a property of the experienced object or a property of the experience of the object?' (Zahavi, 2008: 123). I also think that this is a practical distinction that we make: we warn a child not to touch a fire, for example, because they will get burnt (the fire is hot). But I don't want to debate this here. Rather, I accept the difficulty, and focus on the phenomenological character of peak and optimal experiences. Note also, that Csikszentmihalyi's subjects were involved in a research project using the Experience Sampling Method (see below footnote 1), the keeping of diaries and regular reports about what was going on for them. This, on the whole, rules out the possibility of spontaneity, because the aim and purpose was to report on and collate feelings during the research.

On the other hand, experiences of awe and wonder and sometimes the numinous, are cross-cultural, some from within religious traditions and some without, with or without drugs, regardless of place or time. Their characteristics include momentary loss of a sense of time and space, a feeling of oneness with everything, and then, a feeling that something important, something deeply transformative has taken place which entails a feeling of elevation from the mundane; and perhaps even to the satisfaction of a life goal or the practice of a way of being not previously experienced. However, experiences of awe, wonder, the numinous can be uplifting or shocking: people can be terrified, or people can be elated. The recent interest in awe, and its relationship to mental health and how to live better testifies to this (Baird, 2020; Guan, 2019; Kristjansson, 2016; Rudd et al., 2012).

We need to acknowledge that allusion to awe and wonder, however, is not new. The history of Western mysticism can be read as a map of subjects experiencing awe through their encounters with the Divine. Traceable to the Common Testament, for example, in Moses' encountering Yahweh God in the burning bush, where he could not look on the holy face of the Divine, awe and wonder enter human history as human experience. Jesus' speaking with his father Yahweh God, Saul's blinding on the way to Damascus, and the whole Gospel of John are further examples of biblical awe and wonder (Wansbrough, 1985). Julian of Norwich, John of the Cross, Teresa of Avila, through to the Metaphysical poets all recorded their experiences of the Other, that is to say, the Divine Other. The Buddhist experience of enlightenment, the Sufi Whirling Dervish, Aldous Huxley's *Doors of Perception* likewise point to states of consciousness which are transformative, insightful, but do not always involve a transcendent Other and highlight that experience is available to us that is not part of everyday experience.

And at the end of the nineteenth century, William James' *Varieties of Religious Experience* appeared, followed in the twentieth century by Evelyn Underhill's *Mysticism: A Study of the Nature and Development of Man's Spiritual Consciousness*, and Rudolph Otto's *The Idea of the Holy*. These three helped to establish mystical experience as a category for analysis. The developing interest in Eastern religions and philosophies during the late nineteenth and early twentieth centuries also brought into focus the extensive repertoire of experiences across India, China, Tibet, and Japan. And now into the twenty-first century, with or without religion, people have continued to report and write about awe, wonder, and personal transformation through apparently other-worldly experiences. This catching sight of Otherness considered as an alternative to or an enhancing of, our everyday way of being in the world can be salvific; a life can be changed by the human ability to see things differently, to seeing possibilities in trauma and sadness, poverty, and strife. We can feel incredibly well-disposed to our fellow creatures and enraptured by our surroundings. In these activities, the feeling of oneness suggests the collapsing of boundaries and a re-affirmation of our union with the world in which we are living and participating in this moment. Art, Beauty, and Nature are the grounding of oneness.

What we have here, then, is an idea of the transformative potential that phenomenological experience can bring to us, through attentiveness, through seeing differently, through change and reorientation towards the world. In this book, I am going to focus on spontaneous experience occasioned by immersion in the world, the role of consciousness in this, and Nature, Beauty, and Art. But first, some remarks about consciousness and neuroscience, and the subject/object distinction.

My brain is registering the touch of my fingers on the keyboard as I type and my eyes are watching what I do, bringing light-filled awareness to me. It feels and seems as if I am actually looking out of my head and not from my fingers or my toes or my buttocks that sense that I am seated. This suggests that I am a system or series of networks, all of which work together to produce a 'centre' of awareness that I can identify as myself. In this case, the cold surface of the refrigerator can be regarded as given, just as my experiencing of the cold surface is given through my touch. Many phenomenologists would argue that this is the case for the furniture of the world, and for other people. Importantly, it is not only the world and its objects that are given: I am given to myself in my first person experience, even if I am not given as an object. Whether or not I am or can be an object to myself is another area of philosophical debate. What this analysis alludes to, however is the distinctness yet, the interdependency, at times, of objects that come into my, or anyone's experiential range, and my or anyone's own subjectivity. This is a significant distinction that can help to overcome an everyday philosophical tendency to move always from our individual selves, to a world separate from us. But the world always precedes and engenders our individual existences since the world stands outside us as pre-given. And the world is not just only any old pre-given: as well as ontologically prior to, it is also necessary for our on-going being. Yet we have the extraordinary capacity to experience ourselves as beyond, above, apart from, the natural or ecological environment.

All of these experiences are embedded in, and generated from our bodies, in particular our nervous systems and our brains. Kounios and Beeman remark that

> Much has been written purporting to explain how insight works and how you can make it work better. Almost all of it is based on opinions and informal observations rather than on scientifically established facts … But there is a more complete approach – a scientific approach. Science finishes the job by putting opinions and observations to the test where possible … Techniques such as functional resonance imaging (fMRI) and high density encephalography (EEG) have enabled us to explore the brain in ways that elucidate how we perceive, remember think, feel-–and have insights … Combined with the behavioral research methods of cognitive psychology, brain-imaging studies have revealed new and unexpected aspects of insight that would not have been apparent in measuring a person's behavior alone.
>
> *Kounios and Beeman, 2015: 5*

It is true that FMRI and EEG, along with cognitive psychology, can help to *elucidate* aspects of insight precisely because this technology is looking into our material bodies. But this is elucidation, not explanation, and appears to me to depend on the assumption that the brain is the answer to questions about consciousness. The difference between elucidation (making clear) and explanation (perhaps causal, perhaps ontological) is critical here. And ultimately, a subject must always make a report on her behaviour, say what's going on, in order to back up or confirm what is happening when the fMRI and EEG lights register. And correlation between subjects' report and scientific imaging is correlation and nothing more. Correlation is not identity. Why this happens in the first place remains to be explained: what is it about these firings that produce conscious experience?

And this brings me back to the context of my project: human beings in Nature. Some of the experiences, the aha moments, eureka insights, peak and optimal experiences, can never be captured by scientific imaging precisely because they occur outside a laboratory or experimental conditions. We cannot say that they are all one, although we can say that they are all phenomenological, what they are like, what their effects are, and so on. And the kind of science about which Kounios and Beeman and the kind of work done by Maslow and Csikszentmihalyi attempt to replicate what happens in Nature. The laboratory, important as it is, brackets the world in its efforts to replicate that world. And perhaps that is needed, certainly it is. Ultimately, we return to Nature, to the world. Elucidation is wonderful. But it is not the full story and not an explanation.

In his essay, 'Contemporary Aesthetics and the Neglect of Natural Beauty', Ronald Hepburn remarks that 'we are in nature (Hepburn's spelling of 'Nature')) and a part of nature; we do not stand over against it as over against a painting on a wall' (Hepburn, 1966: 290). In 'Trivial and serious in aesthetic appreciation of nature' Hepburn further emphasises this point of view when he asserts:

> If it trivializes to see nature in terms of ready-made, standard "views," so does it also to see oneself merely as the detached viewer – or indeed as a noumenally free and rational ego. There is a deepening of seriousness when I realise that I am myself one with, part of, the nature over-against me … the energies, regularities, contingencies of nature are the energies, principles and contingencies that sustain my own embodied life and my own awareness. Nature may be "other" to us, but we are no less connatural with it.
>
> *Hepburn in Kemal and Gaskell, 1993: 69*

Hepburn's point has been echoed often enough, that we are in and part of Nature. Yet positioning human animals as somehow outside Nature is exemplified in moral, political, and economic decisions made by individuals, groups, governments, and businesses who refuse, for example, to acknowledge that human beings as creative, transformative animals affect their Natural world just as the transformative actions of ants, and birds do. In acknowledgement of Hepburn I call these two views, respectively, the in-part of and the over-against views but back to this in a moment.

Perhaps the practice of science is over-against Nature but how that can ever be the case is extraordinarily difficult, if not impossible, to see. The intellect and reason are as much in Nature as anything else. And the intellect, reason, *and* the emotions are each aspects of the ability and capacity to transcend. In my view that we can transcend, lift ourselves out of the mucky concerns of reason and emotion does not entail that we are not part of Nature. Indeed, the mystery of life and Nature are encapsulated in the ability to transcend. Whatever we do, we are alway in-part ontological and this very 'in-part' enables the phantasy of over-against simply because we do what we can do. And this can, and does, raise some difficult problems. I hope to deal with some of those problems through this book.

Notes

1 Dickens (1906).
2 By 'phenomenology' I mean what it's like to be something, how things seem to us. Intrinsic to my use is the idea that we can bracket the everyday, and learn. I take phenomenology to be partly about method about method, that is to say, 'phenomenology' refers to the role consciousness plays in our apprehending and theorising the world and what we *do* with our understanding and how we develop and apply our theory. This can (and should) change over time.
3 https://biblehub.com/greek/3689.htm
4 Here, I acknowledge the research scholarship of Zahavi (2016) and Sparrow (2014).

5 Of many things … and especially what and who we are, and how we are connected with Nature and that our Lives depend on it. See Sparrow (2017).

6 See, for example, William James (1902), Jantzen (1995), and Almond (1982).

7 The apparent absence of materiality in the production of sound – the human voice for example–overlooks the materiality of the human body. Music is essentially material because it is both made by and available as sound to us, because of our embodiment.

8

> The Experience Sampling Method (ESM) is a research procedure for studying what people do, feel, and think during their daily lives. not, It consists in asking individuals to provide systematic self-reports at random occasions during the waking hours of a normal week. Sets of these self-reports from a sample of individuals create an archival file of daily experience. Using this file, it becomes possible to address such questions as these: How do people spend their time? What do they usually feel like when engaged in various activities? How do men and women, adolescents and adults, disturbed and normal samples, differ in their daily psychological states?
>
> *Csikszentmihalyi, 2014: 21*

1

EXISTENTIAL EXPERIENCE AND EPIPHANY

In my Introduction, I cited Kounios' and Beeman's judgement about insight and eureka moments. In their view, opinions and informal observations are inadequate. What is needed is scientifically established facts. Recall that this is what they said:

> Much has been written purporting to explain how insight works and how you can make it work better. Almost all of it is based on opinions and informal observations rather than on scientifically established facts.
>
> *supra p. 10*

While science might illuminate some things, it is not an explanation of everything. Scientific facts might underpin what happens in the world, but these facts point to the realities of which most of us are not aware, and do not experience. One of the things that seems, then, to me to be missing from this claim is experience. What we experience is different from what *causes* that experience. That is why I think that an appeal to quantum physics ultimately fails in the case of Buddhism and consciousness. There might be some comparison, even illumination, but there is no explanation or direct *experience* of the subatomic, microscopic, world underlying what goes on at the macroscopic level. The explanation, causal or otherwise, no matter how illuminating of any of our experiences is not the same as what we experience. Knowing that certain areas of my brain light up when I speak or have a particular idea does not affect that knowing or having of an idea: I cannot direct my brain processes, even though I can direct my mind, for example, in concentrating only on one thing.

Recall also, that I consider insight, eureka moments, peak, and optimal *experiences* as phenomenological *experiences*, and that they belong to a family, broadly speaking, of *transformative* experiences. Experience, and the record of experience is a major contributor to the literature of such transformative moments, indeed the foundation. So

DOI: 10.4324/9780429022975-2

I now want to introduce some of those experiences as they have been recorded in various narratives. There is no scientific data around them precisely because they are not scientific data. And one wonders about the relationship between what I consider to be foundational material and what is established in a laboratory: are they the very same thing? Would areas of the brain light up in the same way? How could we know?

Experience as Seeing; Seeing as Experience: Some Preliminary Remarks

In his discussion of Friedrich Nietzsche's *The Birth of Tragedy*, Carl Jung quotes Friedrich Schiller's *Ode to Joy* and writes:

> This is Dionysian expansion. It is a flood of overpowering universal feeling which bursts forth irresistibly, intoxicating the senses like the strongest wine. It is intoxication in the highest sense of the word.
>
> In this state the psychological function of sensation whether it be sensory or affective, participates to the highest degree. It is an extraversion of all those feelings which are inextricably bound up with sensation, for which reason we call it feeling-sensation. What breaks out in this state has more the character of pure affect, something instinctive and blindly compelling, that finds specific expression in an affection of the bodily sphere.
>
> *Jung, 1990: 144*

Now consider this. In *Pilgrim at Tinker Creek* Annie Dillard writes a tender, evocative description of her experience at a gas station in Nowhere, Virginia, where the sun is setting and where she 'has hazarded into a new corner of the world, an unknown spot, a Brigadoon'. She sits on the curb and drinks her coffee and fondles a beagle puppy, while gazing at the splendour of the mountains. She portrays this experience in meticulous, appreciative, detail. 'The air cools; the puppy's skin is hot. I am more alive than all the world' she writes. But then a revelation comes to her:

> This is it, I think, this is it, right now, the present, this empty gas station, here, this western wind, this tang of coffee on the tongue, and I am patting the puppy, I am watching the mountain. And the second I verbalize this awareness in my brain, I cease to see the mountain or feel the puppy. I am opaque, so much black asphalt. But at the same second I know I've lost it, I also realize that the puppy is still squirming on his back under my hand. Nothing has changed for him.
>
> *Dillard, 1974 (2013): 78 ff*

It is clear that something profound happened to Annie Dillard, something she did not intend, and that she later recorded. Annie Dillard's experience echoes the pure affect of which Carl Jung speaks. But Annie Dillard elaborates her experience and makes a direct comparison between what we might think of as pure experience and narrative experience. Words were not part of the moment and interfered with, disrupted what happened to her. For her, that present moment was wordless. The introduction of words through the verbalising in her brain fractured the full mobilisation of her senses: 'and the second I verbalize this awareness in my brain, I cease to see the mountain or the puppy ...'. While she is 'in' the experience, she is touched by the Natural world in a way that takes her beyond words, beyond language, where words are unnecessary. It is a non-narrative moment. It is also a moment deeply connected to individuation, because it is a moment of palpable withdrawal of projections. But almost immediately, language intervened, and functioned to separate her from the experience in which she was fully sensuously alive without being cognitively self-conscious. Once she started to think about what was going on for her, she was brought into cognitive self-consciousness; she became an observer, as if she were a stranger, separate from the Natural world. In other words, verbalisation and narrative became divisive as self-conscious awareness kicked in once more.[1] Dillard remarks that it 'is ironic that the one thing that all religions recognize as separating us from our creator—our very self-consciousness—is also the one thing that divides us from our fellow creatures' (Dillard, 1974 (2013): 79–80). This is the crux of what this book is about.

Earlier in her text, Annie Dillard remarked that seeing 'is of course very much a matter of verbalization'. She explained that 'a running description of the present' is necessary for her to know what is happening. And she says of this realisation that she is like 'a blind man at the ball game' who needs a radio. But, she says, there is another kind of seeing that involves letting go. 'The difference between the two ways of seeing is the difference between walking with and without a camera' (Dillard, 1974 (2013): 33). The letting go towards which she gestures is the letting go of self-consciousness and of language about which she subsequently speaks. Thus it seems to me that in Dillard's description, we have the crux of what I am calling the transformative phenomenal experience. This is a non-narrative existential moment: full attention, absorption through the senses, absence of self-consciousness, absence of language. During this period, it seems as if there is no experience of subject and object.

This is an important point about how language constructs us as subjects of experience and the what, the objects of that experience. I shall come back to this point shortly. What we can see in Dillard's remarks is that with the return of language, experience changes. Language or its absence marks off what and how something is experienced. We might wonder if the cognitive mind always involves language? If we tune into what Annie Dillard writes *after* the event, we might be inclined to say that it does not. If cognition and awareness are allies, or complement each other, and if there are various ways of seeing as John Berger also suggests, then language takes a back seat in at least some of our understanding of cognition and experience. What we can say is that Annie Dillard's experience had a quality which many of our experiences do not have, merely because we are perpetual narrators, just as Dillard suggests she is. In this case, however, she was, to some degree, *fully* her senses. She seemed to experience a seamless connection with the world 'outside' her. She found herself in that world, without narration and, paradoxically, without separation. She felt a wholeness and oneness with something greater than herself that in her gross everyday life she does not usually experience.

In the opening chapter of *Ways of Seeing* John Berger says, '(s)eeing comes before words. The child looks and recognizes before it can speak'. Like Annie Dillard, John Berger is also invoking different senses of 'seeing'. Berger says,

> But there is also another sense in which seeing comes before words. It is seeing which establishes our place in the surrounding world; we explain that world with words, but words can never undo the fact that we are surrounded by it.
>
> *Berger, 1972: 7*

As we have seen above, Carl Jung recognises a version of this as a Dionysian moment, and he also speaks of 'seeing differently' in the case of transformation experiences: change occurs in an experiencing subject rather than in an object's being experienced (Suzuki, 1964: 17). What is clear is that Annie Dillard, John Berger, and Carl Jung distinguish ways of seeing that alter how we experience ourselves and the worlds we inhabit. Carl Jung further distinguishes different psychological states and affects (Dionysian and Apollinian) and unconscious type-preferences: introverted, extraverted, intuition, sensation, judgement, thinking, feeling (what becomes the basis of Myers–Briggs type indicators) which can be mapped onto varieties of these experiences.

For the moment, let me concentrate on the importance of John Berger's allusion to seeing as a pre-linguistic activity. He also maintains that what we know and believe affects what we see and that we always see something/s. In other words, seeing is a direct and intentional response to something outside ourselves. The absence of language and then its intrusive nature during Annie Dillard's experience connects in a kind of reversal, with John Berger's comments. Does she revert to the pre-linguistic 'state' (I am not sure what to call it) to which John Berger refers? And Carl Jung notes the psychological effect of seeing differently in transformation experiences. So 'seeing' turns out to be a multifaceted dimension of our worldly experience with our immersion directly affected with or without language. But the *momentary* absence of language brings us to a different mode of perception and experience. What this suggests is that the presence of language, the propensity many of us have to be narrators of our lives, leaves little room to experience either ourselves or the world through our senses alone. If John Berger is right, and I believe he is, language obscures ourselves and the world to us, as well as functioning to bring the world to us.

Dillard's fondling of the dog and her gazing at the mountain did not involve her self-conscious mind but involved her conscious awareness nonetheless. Her experience was one of sensual engagement that, in theory, could be open to anyone. I say 'in theory' because many of us as I have just mentioned, like Dillard, routinely narrate our own lives as we walk through our days. Narration has become the centre of our being, as individuals and as whole communities: it is integral to psychotherapy, to use of social media, to friendship and history making. We seem *not* to be able to do without words: the narrative areas of our brains always seem to be switched on.[2] Experiences like Dillard's would sweep us away from words and narration, but taken up as we are with the world and ourselves, they may never happen.[3] And if they do we may think what has happened is mysterious, an aberration, so discount whatever happened and not think about it or yearn for its recurrence. Furthermore, if it were possible, it would be very interesting to see through fMRI and EEG, what happens with the language areas of the brain during such experiences, *away from a laboratory* (and how is this possible?).

Turning out or in as the case may be, away from the constant narrative we take to be so necessary for our being, and into which we automatically slip, has the potential to bring with it, ontological novelty, a different understanding, an insight, clarity, an answer to a problem. I hold that language *adds* to our experience of the world without being the primary source of that experience. Rather, our senses, *and the world itself*, are that source. Language frames our senses and sensuous experience of the world in light of our primary, sensuous immersion, which is the genesis of our experience. Language in the form of narrativity is integral to our selves, but is not their totality; narrative is part of our biographical record but is not its totality.[4] The body does keep the score (van der Kolk, 2015).

We take our ability to narrate for granted and what we take for granted can have a levelling effect on our psyches: surprise, awe, and wonder can be compromised by immersion in the taken for granted, the ordinariness of the everyday which many of us inhabit. Yet some of us, like Dillard, do have moments where we experience something quite different from the everyday: we see not ordinariness, but *extra*-ordinariness. We are changed by what seems to be a sudden revelation; our lives are given a different or new meaning; we experience an existential transformation in a moment, or in a series of moments. I refer to these moments as psychic epiphanies which are phenomenological experiences, for the depths into which we are drawn and from which we subsequently emerge alter, profoundly, our consciousness or ourselves as individuals and as community members. We are existentially transformed. And this is how I think of what happened to/with Annie Dillard.

So this is the point I want to make here: we take for granted the world and how it has been constructed for us through language and experience and then how we have constructed it through narrative. Yet sometimes language and those constructions drop away, and we find ourselves in an almost 'magical' world of the senses, a world in which boundaries seem to have collapsed and we feel a sense of oneness with where we are. For some of us, this might mean we 'accidentally' catch hold, visually, of a rising moon, or a rainbow (or even a motor car accident), or we might hear a piece of music with a different ear. Importantly, this can be the occasion of transformation, of profound change. Something we have not seen or experienced before happens. Sensory consciousness prevails as the body lets go its dependency on language for what and how we experience.

Annie Dillard's is an experience in which seeing is the catalyst, but in which she, like John Berger, also alerts us to different meanings of 'seeing' and 'sight' and their effects on consciousness. Her experience is not unique. In *My Stroke of Insight*, Jill Bolte Taylor relates such a time (Taylor, 2009), H.G Wells mentions such moments (Wells, 1993) as do mystics and poets (Hildegard & Fox, 1987; Oliver, 1992).

Consider, also, this passage from Barbara Hepworth, describing her relationship with both Nature and her sculpture:

> I was the figure in the landscape and every sculpture contained to a greater or lesser degree the ever-changing forms and contours embodying my own response to a given position in the landscape. What a different shape and 'being' one becomes lying on the sand with the sea almost above from when standing against the wind on a high sheer cliff with seabirds circling patterns below one; and again what a contrast between the form one feels within oneself sheltering near some great rocks or reclining in the sun on the grass-covered rocky shapes which make the double spiral of Pendour or Zennor Cove; this transformation of essential unity with land and seascape, which derives from all the sensibilities, was for me a voyage of exploration. There is no landscape without the human figure: it is impossible for me to contemplate pre-history in the abstract. Without the relationship of man and his land the mental image becomes a nightmare.
>
> *Hepworth, 1952*

Hepworth's realisation of the association between Nature and her Art, between her position relative to the sea and the foreshore, and her Art is illuminating.[5] For she notes that there is an 'essential unity with land and seascape, which derives from all sensibilities', an explorative voyage. Her remark that there was a transformation derivative of all sensibilities underlines the centrality of our senses to all of our experiences, above all to Natural environment and Art.

Hepworth does not say that narrative is accompanying her experience, and we cannot tell if this was the case. Rather she focuses on the relationship between herself as an embodied, sensuous, being and the land/sea. She appears to have realised that the shape of her sculptural works and the shapes of land/sea have an inextricable connection with one another; not a reciprocal connection, but rather an aesthetic connection which is derived from the experience of Nature through the senses. From her description, Hepworth sounds as if there is no mental space for narrative as she is full of sensory awareness, which she later inscribes into her sculpture. An ordinary beach, an ordinary experience? But a Jungian Dionysian experience?

The answer to this query is both yes and no. We need to acknowledge that there are elements of the very ordinary in Barbara Hepworth's and Annie Dillard's accounts. They were not visited by a god, or an angel; there was no earthquake or flash of lightning from the heavens. Indeed, the experiences are almost cemented in the non-remarkable: seashore, cliffs, cars, gas stations, pets, birds, and sunlight are a regular part of everyday life. But there is something going on in such experiences that make them extra-ordinary, make them remarkable in fact, in spite of their ordinariness, their everyday qualities—or even because of their ordinariness. Their importance lies in the wordless immersion experience, in the bracketing/suspension/abandonment of narration as the senses are captured, maybe even enraptured, by a Beauty that shines through and initiates the experiences. And, subsequently, Beauty illuminates the text, the sculpture, the poetic turn of phrase, the evocation of the experience through narrative and three-dimensional Art that later acts as a memento of the moments of transformed ordinariness. In these cases, experience of the present moment springs consciousness into another mode: consciousness, engrossed in the senses, journeying away from narrative, even if momentarily, alters itself to speak to itself, and, then, later, to externalise, to speak to us this inner narrative.

Furthermore, and this is of great importance, the transformation of the ordinary experience is to do with human perception, with how we perceive and how we feel the world: our psyches change. An ordinary experience is transformed by an alteration in or of our consciousnesses, we are in an existential moment, where, ultimately we *see* differently.

Seeing differently is intrinsic to many psychological and religious practices. Change which involves seeing differently or achieving union with a divine force is sought for peace, tranquillity, for knowledge of the arcane, for a different way of being in the world. In the 'Foreword' to D.T. Suzuki's *An Introduction to Zen Buddhism* Carl Jung wonders if there is anything in the West like the Zen experience of *satori*. He points out that the '(t)he mere thought that there is a tremendous psychological difference between consciousness of the existence of an object and the "consciousness of the consciousness" of an object borders on a subtlety which can scarcely be answered'. He goes on to note that it is in Indian Yoga and Chinese Buddhism that states of consciousness were addressed as limiting and from which one needed to be freed. Yet Jung notes that Western mystical

> texts are full of instructions as to how a man can and must release himself from the "I-ness" (*Ichhafttikeit*) of his consciousness, so that through the knowledge of his being he may raise himself above it and reach the inward (godlike).
>
> *Suzuki, 1964: 16*

His focus on consciousness across these traditions leads him to acknowledge that change is a matter of deliberate, conscious direction; indeed a new consciousness is a product of decision and practice.

But his remark that it 'could be objected that consciousness in itself was not changed, but only consciousness of something ... (but that) it is not merely a different picture or object that is described, but rather the experience of a transformation... It is not that something different is seen, but that one sees differently' (Suzuki, 1964: 17) is relevant here. While the origins of seeing differently might not be the same in all cases, Jung's remark gives us a way of approaching existential moments that are epiphanic. And, interestingly, Zen Buddhism provides some very fruitful insights into what goes on.

In the religious traditions and philosophies across the planet, we can find accounts that resonate with and pre-date what Jung is talking about here. As he notes, a search for the divine, a search for enlightenment, and also a search for ultimate meaning are some of the themes of philosophical and religious quests, and in hagiography. The Greek and Roman Stoics and Epicureans are the basis of the European tradition (Hadot, 1995, 1998). A saint is made according to her efforts, her success, her failure, her realisation. But this immediately highlights the importance of deliberate seeking out, and its difference from the spontaneity of the existential moments with which I am concerned. Nevertheless, we can learn from philosophical and religious insight and conversion or illumination in cases where narration, or particular forms of narration, become bracketed in religious practices.

However, Jung also notes that there are limitations when it comes to comparing *satori* with Christian religious experience: there are various 'degrees and types' of such experience. Only those that exhibit '"emptiness" or "release"' are related closely to satori. With Zen, he points out, the individualism and the 'iconoclastic attitude of many of the masters' suggests its heterodox and paradoxical nature (Suzuki, 1964: 19). Here, we might explore more closely what it is that contributes to these qualities of Zen.

A recurrent theme in Zen Buddhism is the overcoming of dualistic or binary thinking, in other words, the overcoming of logic, the dissolution of the subject and object distinction. According to D.T. Suzuki

> Your mind is above all forms; it is free and quiet and sufficient; it eternally stamps itself in your six senses and four elements ... Hush the dualism of subject and object, forget both, transcend the intellect, sever yourself from understanding, and directly penetrate deep into the Buddha-mind; outside this there are no realities.
>
> *Suzuki, 1964: 46*

As will become evident through this book, I reject this Buddhist conception of reality in which there is no reality outside the Buddha-mind. In my view this is a radical anthropocentrism—human consciousness is the determinant of what exists as a content only of consciousness. The meditation process supposes that consciousness 'contains' reality, viz. that the fleetingness of sensations and perceptions reveals how the world actually is, Suzuki's 'outside this there are no realities'. However, I do agree that epistemological dualism of subject and object is embedded in logic, in the words, in the phrases, in the rational thinking with and in which we operate. *But we could not live a life without such logic.* However, according to Buddhist traditions, liberation from this logic is the key to acquiring 'an entirely new point of view whereby to look into the mysteries of life and the secrets of nature'. Suzuki explains that in Zen Buddhism, one must break up the 'tyranny of name and logic' and that through the process of transcending dualities an altered perception, viz. a change in consciousness, the 'soul is thus made whole, perfect, and filled with bliss' (Suzuki, 1964: 59–61).

The transcending of logic and attaining of a different point of view requires a suspension of narrative but for Zen Buddhists, this is not so simply the case. Something different is going on. Rather, it is a matter of seeing differently from the first. Suzuki says that 'Zen wishes to storm this citadel of topsy-turvydom and to show that we live psychologically or biologically and not logically' (Suzuki, 1964: 64).

The puzzles presented to Zen students are meant to challenge logical thinking, which, through a process of reasoning—that is to say a narrative—would normally be dealt with. How one understands the holding of a spade and yet not holding it, cannot though, be reasoned. We cannot come up with a narrative that can explain this contradiction; we cannot, with reason, understand. In order to apprehend its intent, that is, its push to make one think differently, even to not think, one must suspend the talking mind.

Yet the puzzles, the *koan*, posed by Zen masters, sometimes require a spoken answer.[6] To the question, then, 'What is the Buddha?' Tozan gave the answer, 'Three pounds of flax'. This spoken answer is not, however, a narrative, and what is more, a narrative containing metaphysical assumptions. It is a response from 'inmost consciousness as water flows out of a spring', as Suzuki points out. Zen, he says, is not a form of pantheism, nor any form of philosophy (Suzuki, 1964: 79). The response to a puzzle lies in intuition and in the senses, and not in logic; inmost consciousness is not a logical domain. Rather, it is a seat of insight which is harnessed in spite of logic and which will lead to the opening of one's mind without narrative. Tentatively, this is John Berger's pre-linguistic realm. 'Solving' a *koan* requires insight, an alteration of consciousness without narrative. As in Annie Dillard's realisation that she ongoingly narrates her life and that she can be captured by her senses in wonder and new seeing, so with Zen *koan* solving. You don't get there by reason, or even by words: you get there by letting go, by seeing differently. I follow this up in Chapter 2 where I consider how we might understand the notion of change in relations to our thinking of ourselves as selves.

Seeing in Nature

Carlo Rovelli writes that we are

> an integral part of the world which we perceive; we are not external observers. We are situated within it ... We are made up of the same atoms and the same light signals as are exchanged between pine trees in the mountains and stars in the galaxies ... Nature is our home, and in nature, we are at home. This strange, multicoloured and astonishing world which we explore – where space is granular, time does not exist, and things are nowhere is not something that estranges us from our true selves, for this is only what our natural curiosity reveals to us about the place of our dwelling. About the stuff of

> which we ourselves are made. We are made of the same stardust of which all things are made, and when we are immersed in suffering or when we are experiencing intense joy we are being nothing other than what we can't help be; a part of our world.
>
> *Rovelli, 2015: 64, 77–78*

Carlo Rovelli is a scientist. His comment, beautifully worded and evocative, pinpoints the place of humans amongst the stars. He is talking about the cosmos, and he is talking about Nature, that of which we are part. Perhaps we are not familiar with the stars or with particle physics. What we are familiar with, though, is the idea of home, and 'home' for us, is the Earth, with sky, trees, rivers, rainbows, our dwellings, where we belong. We can identify with Nature, that of which we are small fragments, but which remains separate, nonetheless from us: Nature is greater than we. Our cultures and reason are products of Nature, conceived of as the totality of the cosmos. Nature is the provider, the originary source for all that we make or break, and all that is distant from us and utterly intimate to us, in every sense. Nature is inescapable as both the condition of our being, and its on-going ground. This is surely a consequence of Rovelli's view.

We humans are living beings in a world of other living beings, inheritors of the stars to which we all return when we die. We are not, fundamentally, immortal souls who will survive this life and go on to a better or worse post-mortem life. Claims like this can be found in many philosophies and religions. Such claims are an invitation to a metaphysical debates and blunders that are inescapable when we persist in repeating metaphysics that do not countenance recent research into the brain and the nervous system, and that do not place us right smack bang in Nature, that do not acknowledge the outdatedness of historically embedded metaphysics (Koch, 2012, 2019). The splendour of being is not that we are something other than what we are, indeed what we appear to be: it is that we are as we are, and that is, part of the Natural world the world of the stars and the Earth.

What we *really* are is not an embodied soul say, a something that survives bodily death. We are fragments of original creation, conscious beings, part of Nature. And that is the greatest joy and mystery we can realise. We are each an on-going living awareness, specifically a self-consciousness. If we wanted to persist with using aspirational language of heaven and eternity, we need to view this as evocative and symbolic rather than metaphysical or ontological. Thus we would need to understand 'soul', 'spirit', 'true being', as tropes that point to experience but experience that we do not fully understand. Once we do this, we might broach the non-narrative world of being. From this perspective, the terms would not apply to anything divine as theologians and religious pundits might say; and they would not refer to an internal observer or stillness as yogis might say (and is so often repeated by yoga teachers across the world). Rather, we would hold that awareness, and our self-consciousness comes to us through our brains, soft grey and white squishy living matter, electrically and chemically charged, supplied with blood, that is constantly active: were our brains, and thus our awareness, to become still, we would be dead. We would need to acknowledge the mystery of this connection between brain and symbolic system. And we would also want to hold, that awareness, and self-consciousness, are activity, but are not reducible to that activity (Koch, 2020).

At this point, you might ask, 'But just what is this awareness, this self-consciousness, and how are these related to experience?' As I have already indicated, I cannot answer this question. However, as humans we are in Nature and we make Art and Beauty.[7] Indeed, our awareness of ourselves in community, in environments, Natural or built, has a direct impact on our self—and Other-understanding. As we mature, our personal and private awareness necessitates a movement away—out—from the internalised consciousnesses we might take ourselves to be. Art 'out-there' affects consciousness/self-consciousness 'in-here'. And this applies not only to the visual, but embraces the polysemic notions of seeing. Music, song, verse, in other words, the auditory, for example, can manifest as the generative force of a life changed by Art, and enhance our being, beyond our ordinariness.[8]

We might also ponder the relevance of bringing Nature and Carlo Rovelli's views into the picture. After all, science seems a long way from Art.... But consider this. On the whole, in the Western world and since the Industrial Revolution, we have more and more lost the world of Nature. We have lost Nature in many ways. We have filled the air with industrial pollutants, filled the seas with human muck that has acidified their waters and made them uninhabitable for many aquatic species. We have cleared land to such an extent that the biodiversity once present, has shrunk, and shrunk (Eniscuola, 2020; IPCC, 2021; WHO, 2020). And many of us have lost Nature to ourselves: we live in vast concrete and tarred cities and our souls are inspired by what we have made and not by what was once there for us, uninvited. Computerisation, and social media in the twenty-first century, have enacted an enormous crime on ourselves in Nature, no matter what their benefits. We have not learned to live in Nature but seek, always, to pretend that we can live above Nature. For many of us, and for those with power, influence and money, profit, being the first and the best, and immediacy are more important than anything else. Respect and compassion for each other, and preservation, conservation, and admission that we are part of Nature are minimal considerations.

So Carlo Rovelli's scientific understanding provides the broad brush strokes, the background against which we might reflect on the loss of Nature. No matter what, we cannot avoid or evade Nature. And his remarks that we are continuous with the cosmos are especially poignant as a jolting reminder that we are subject to ancient laws and history beyond either our control or full understanding. Our senses, both conscious and unconscious, are a direct and deepest link to the Natural world.

Consider this as well .... There is more than sight, always, for example, in seeing. We encounter the world through touch: seeing is both touching and being touched by the world. Our senses, particularly our sense of sight, rely on light in the world; both light and the world are other to us, yet are simultaneously crucial to our being in the world. My being a seeing subject and (the possibility of) my being seen (as subject, as object, or as prey) suggest the dialogical nature of seeing, for this visual dialogue invokes community or otherness of fellow humans—and of other animals. One can imagine the plethora of possibilities here: the seer is seen and the seer is the seen: as members of community, we are all potentially both the seeing subject and seen subject/object. There is a visual reciprocity, an exchange, between the world and me. The reciprocity, however, is always mediated by something else: by touch.

Of our human senses, touch is the most ancient for us each: touch is the primary sense, the primary form of consciousness. On this account, consciousness is engendered by touch and is not something that is simply limited to the head: response, of any kind, is, fundamentally, touch. We touch with our fingers and toes, we feel the texture of clothing on our bodies, and our lips kiss the world. But even in very basic, non-human instances of consciousness as awareness and response this is the case: light touches the sunflower, water touches the fish, the snake touches the grass. For humans, our first sense, even though we may not be self-consciously aware of it, is the touch implicit in our living within the intimacy of the female body. That sensuous initiation is what we carry with us through our lives, albeit our on-going memorial ignorance of this fact. Hence I am understanding 'touch' in two related ways: firstly as the individual sense which is, secondly, simultaneously present in all of the senses (sight, sound, taste, smell). Sound, the sound of the voice, for example, which involves the vibration of the membranes of the ear is the touch of vibrational waves against the flesh. In short, touch is the primary sense upon which all other senses depend and is pivotal in our development and maturation. Everything about us, including our creativity, is engendered by touch, by our senses.[9] Like 'sight' and 'seeing', 'touch' is polysemic.

Touch, then, brings us to the world and the world to us. Our presence to the Natural world, Beauty, and Art depends on our senses. Through the blue of the sky, the shape of cloud, the sea, rivers, mountains and trees, fresh air, dawn and dusk, stars and flowers, even trauma, pain and unhappiness, our senses are continually and continuously mobilised, as we find ourselves and our origins. We cannot avoid this. Our individual generation and subsequent growth in the female body, followed by nurturing and development, is both Natural and social *but is fundamentally sensuous.*

This brings us to our physical origins and to our experiences that make us human bodies we are. Biology matters as it is the physicality, the material nature of biology that grounds and generates our senses. We *are* our experience, bodies who experience, bodies that are both conscious and self-conscious, bodies that can be mute or speaking. What we write about is, in a robust sense, a report, an interpretative, intricate story and we have seen this in Annie Dillard and Barbara Hepworth as they write about experience in itself without words. Overall, the intricacies, whether they are personal or based on scientific discovery, on empirical work, on seeing the world through various eyes with which humans perceive the world are the very grit of our experience.

The mostly unacknowledged grounding of our very being, of our thinking and intellectual work in general, is our sensuous experience in and of the world. We can, it seems, make our minds go where we want them to by mere fiat, believe what we want to believe and act upon it, with different consequences, both personal and community. While this might always have been the case for some of us, since its development social media has had a significant, instant impact on who and what and how we are. Consider, for instance, Donald Trump's inability to acknowledge the result of the 2020 US election, and the willing believers who accept without question, his declarations about its corrupted outcome, and the consequent attack on the US Capitol in January 2021; or mass protests in Australia and France against community lock-downs to contain Corona virus; or the populist anti-vaxxer movements. We make up lies, fabricate alleged truths without evidence, and ignore alternative views especially when they are contrary to our own. But we can also investigate, research, come up with substantiated theories (although science is always open to revision with new perceptions, interpretations, and insights). All of this involves irrevocably, our senses.

Thus whatever we believe and/or subscribe to, we are bodies in this physical world, subject to its laws. We can take any of these paths, or sometimes one, then the other, but our roaming minds and thus our brains are in our responsive, aware bodies, in this world, now. The impossibility of escaping the fact that we are conscious flesh in the world, in whatever we do, is captured by Juhani Pallasmaa when he remarks,

> (a)rt and architecture are not primarily about aesthetics, as is usually believed but about how to be human in this world … Great works of art and architecture enable us to realize our own humanity, sensitize our experiences, and expand our realm of existential and emotive knowledge.
>
> *Pallasmaa, 2018: 52*

Pallasmaa's comment is salient when one considers the symbolic weight of the Capitol Building in Washington, DC, and the pleas to *stay at home*, the symbolic site of the family, of protection and nurturing.

Let us also note that Carl Jung was at pains to distinguish between the symbolic and other modes of experience and understanding. Sigmund Freud, likewise, emphasised the importance of the symbolic as he developed theories around infant sexuality, and various complexes (like the Oedipus complex). It is an important distinction, one that should not be overlooked because (a) as far as we know the symbolic is unique to human culture and (b) the symbolic in various modes is apparent in every human culture, again a point well made by Jung across his *oeuvre* (Jung, 1967).

Importantly, and this I stress, there is more than Nature and Art at work here. What is central to these experiences, and, subsequently, to the description, is Beauty. Had there not been Beauty, had they not been aware of the exquisite gifts of the Natural world, they would have travelled, and experienced, without really thinking about what was going on, or even more tellingingly, without feeling what was going on. Beauty enveloped Annie Dillard and Barbara Hepworth: theirs were, fundamentally, sensuous experiences; they were enveloped in and by touch. Their senses told them about this world in which they live. They were touched by light and sound, by the air, by the feeling of animal fur and body warmth, by sand and cliff and sea. Touch engaged them with the world.

And how important is touch! Not to be so engaged or to be touched in a loveless, cruel way, is madness and/or death, or exaggerated to the point of sadism, a fact not overlooked by some human practices ("Senate Report on CIA Torture," 2014). Touch involves both toucher and what is touched. Indeed, the whole of our existence is an existence of touching and being touched. Whoever looks, listens, smells, whoever makes love, or creates Beauty in making Art, whoever looks at or hears birds, birdsong, the sound of the ocean, whoever thinks about and/or feels these things, uses this basic symmetry in their encounter with the world, and, indeed with anything. Being alive and being human is about being touched and touching in ways that produce specific effects, exploitation notwithstanding. The same is the case for the making of ugliness: both the beautiful and the ugly co-exists in a sensuous, sensible world.

Sensuous, caring, tender touch, then, brings us to Beauty and to the world in various ways. Touch works us psychologically. Touch creates epiphany, creates existential awareness in a manner that is *non-narrative* and has to do with whom and/or what we are in the world, with whom we assume ourselves to be or whom we would like to be, with heightened awareness of our existence. I stress that this is without an accompanying narrative. These are moments of profound experience. The importance of the non-narrative is critical here, since many of our philosophies and cultures are driven by the belief that narrative is central to modern human identity.[10]

It is precisely because of claims about sight and sound that touch is important. While it is true that most of us depend upon sight and sound, upon seeing and hearing, it is also true that some of us cannot see and hear. There, the sense that is touch—a kiss on the cheek, the stroke of a hand—comes into its own, along with the senses of taste and smell. Helen Keller, who was born with her sight and hearing and lost them through illness when she was two, was at the forefront of living a life that depended on touch, in the form of touch-signing, in spite of her disabilities (American Foundation for the Blind, 2022). The thing is that touch, the physical coming together of bodies, or body and water, or body and sunlight, exemplify the self/other paradigm just as do hearing and sight.

The transformative power—and it is a power—of human ingenuity, skill, and imagination is self-evident when looked at in this way. Perhaps this transformative power is Art or is in Art? And perhaps it is derivative of Nature in the first place, for the beautiful natural setting was what aesthetically framed the whole performance? My writing, and Dillard's, of these experiences *after* suggests performance. However, the drive to write emerges from a pulsing, solid, body experiencing its own consciousness—its immediate memory—in story-telling.

I acknowledge that there are many existential moments that are epiphanic: the insight they bring is profound and life changing, carrying as they do, the experience of being wondrously human in a manner that might not before have been experienced. Thus the existential and the epiphanic are linked in ways that take us deeply into our psyches and into the world. Existential moments can be the occasion of all kinds of transformation, including moral transformation, in which the existential itself becomes the epiphanic. I shall have more to say about this through the work. That said, I argue that non-narrative moments constitute a class of existential moments that fall outside our will to speak, to tell, to talk endlessly about the world and its objects and experiences. Non-narrative moments are moments of change: we change from the compulsive narrator inside our heads, to a wordless conscious presence. Touch is the foundation of this and the foundation of our experience. And the touch of Nature, without words, is our home.

Notes

1 For a discussion of narrative and its role in the constitution of self, see Gray (2016) especially Chapter 2.
2 I cite social media statistics in favour of this. The number of people online and participating in social media outlets, for example, has increased and continues to rise. See https://wearesocial.com/au/blog/2020/02/digital-2020-in-australia-analysis/; www.esafety.gov.au/about-us/research/adults-negative-online-experiences; www.statista.com/statistics/467753/forecast-of-smartphone-users-in-australia/
3 Yoga and meditation students are surprised at wordless moments that might occur during their practice. And some have great difficulty with ever achieving wordless practice (and they give up). I know one yoga teacher who says she has the constant drive to reach for her phone even during yoga practice. So this is not an easy thing for many of us to do. Annie Dillard *did* nothing: she was not expecting what happened to her, so it is a case of spontaneity that falls outside Csikszentmihalyi's optimal experience, yet at the same time, we might want to say that it is, precisely what he is talking about. This does not mean though, that there were not causal factors involved.
4 For a discussion of narrative identity I recommend Paul Ricoeur's essay 'Narrative Identity' which explores various positions (Derek Parfitt in particular) as well as his own. See Ricoeur (1991).
5 I am not sure about her assertion that there is no landscape without the human figure. Does it echo George Berkeley's question, 'If a tree falls in the forest and no-one hears it does it make a sound?' In other words if there is no-one to see the landscape then there is no landscape because the idea of landscape is a human idea? Or is she assuming that there needs to be a human figure in a landscape for it to be a landscape? In that case, human beings are what make landscapes into landscapes which, for me, is counter intuitive. Furthermore, her allusions to contemplating pre-history in the abstract and that the relationship of man and his land is central to a cogent mental image rather than a nightmare (without this image) is problematic for me.
6 According to D.T Suzuki,

> *Ko-an* literally means "a public document" or "authoritative statute" – a term coming into vogue toward the end of the T'ang dynasty. It now denotes some anecdote of an ancient master, or a dialogue between a master and monks, or a statement or question put forward by a teacher, all of which are used as the means for opening one's mind to the truth of Zen.
>
> *Suzuki, 1964: 102*

The *koan* is well known as a puzzle or dilemma that cannot be solved logically.

7 I use the upper case for 'Art', 'Beauty', and 'Nature' to stress their significance as the concepts with which I am working in this book. To be honest, I cannot define them, although I do acknowledge the vast number of words that have been employed in their definition. I believe that many of us actually have an intuitive understanding of their meanings and it is that to which I appeal.

8 I cite personal favourites, the *andante cantabile* from Tchaikovsky's String Quartet I or Leonard Cohen's 'Hallelujah' or the singing of the Australian magpie and butcher bird, or Karl Jenkins' 'Armed Man, Mass for Peace', in favour of this.

9 See Antonio Damasio (2000, 2021), Bessel Van Der Kolk (2015), and Francisco Varela, Evan Thompson, and Eleanor Rosch (2016) all acknowledge this.

10 Narration/narrativity is central to some theories about the selves that we are, and to psychologies. See Ricoeur (1991, 2012) who is a primary proponent of this view.

2

CHANGE

Nature, Beauty, Art

Subject and Object

Wholeness

Epiphanic experiences are characterised by a feeling of wholeness and oneness with the universe. How can this be? The world is *out there* and I have my skin boundary that separates me from that world. While I might agree that I am part of that world, I nonetheless have a separateness that is indisputable from an existential perspective. I live and move in and through the world as an autonomous being just like all the other autonomous beings—people, trees, kangaroos, fish, sunflowers, and amoeba—that are identifiable as separate and separable. The world and autonomous beings are, yes, it is true, intertwined, but at the same time their uniqueness and individuality is what we all experience.

What we can and do experience is different from what might be the case. Carlo Rovelli's acknowledgement that we are of the same material as the stars and as well as research into, and explanations of, what is going on in our brains when we speak, feel excited, happy, or sad, are instances of scientific explanation and not the experiences themselves. As I have just intimated, even if science can explain what is happening, in the end, what is happening, say in the case of consciousness and the brain, is not what we experience. So I want to maintain a distinction between experience and explanation and various kinds of awareness.

This is an interesting and important distinction to make. Jill Bolte Taylor knew what was happening when she had her stroke and even alludes to our being 'aware that we are made up of trillions of cells, gallons of water, and ultimately everything about exists in a constant and dynamic state of activity' (Taylor, 2009: 69). We might wonder just what kind of awareness it is that we have? In Jill Bolte Taylor's case, it seems to me that she was experiencing at least two different kinds of awareness

DOI: 10.4324/9780429022975-3

during her stroke: both phenomenological awareness *and* cognitive awareness. In other words, states of awareness are various.

> I was consciously alert and my perception was that I was in flow. Everything in my visual world blended together, and with every pixel radiating energy we all flowed *en masse*, together as *one*. It was impossible for me to distinguish the physical boundaries between objects because everything radiated with a similar energy … My conscious mind felt so detached from my physical body that I sincerely believed that I would never be able to fit the energy of me back inside this skin, nor ever be able to reengage the intricate networks of my body's cellular and molecular tapestry. I felt suspended between two worlds caught between two perfectly opposite planes of reality.
>
> *Taylor, 2009: 69–73*

Jill Bolte Taylor's experiencing full awareness (loss of boundaries, suspension of time) grounded her cognitive, conscious awareness of what was happening, at least as far as she was able to apply what she believed to be the case at the time. She even raises this question, 'Wasn't it interesting that although I could not talk, understand language, read or write, or even roll my body over, I knew that I was okay?' Given that she could not talk, understand, read, or write, we might wonder about using the term 'cognitive' in relation to her awareness. Her knowing that she was okay, suggests both cognition and emotional reassurance. She says that she saw herself as a 'cellular masterpiece' and perceived herself as 'perfect, whole, and beautiful just the way I was' (Taylor, 2009: 71). She seems to be appealing to some kind of intuitive awareness that she had and if this is the case, then we need to extend our notions of cognition and phenomenological awareness.

Hence it seems reasonable to assume that Jill Bolte Taylor was the subject of awareness in different modes, all of which were connected through her traumatised, and failing, body. Had her body ceased to function completely, she would have died. *Post factum* with the restoration of language, she describes this. And here is a difficulty: did language actually accompany what was happening, or, rather, did she put words to her experience when she could? Since she admits she could not talk or understand, read or write, yet seems to have had cognitive awareness the answer to this question seems clear enough. Thus we need to wonder exactly what constituted her experiencing 'centre' of her being. She notes that she was not unconscious during the stroke, so her consciousness seems to be operating apart from language function. Her feelings of enormity and expansiveness, her not-thinking in language, shifted her to 'taking new pictures of what was going on in the present moment' (Taylor, 2009: 68). She experienced a non-narrative moment, or series of moments.

There are strong similarities between Jill Bolte Taylor's stroke experience, Annie Dillard's moment at the gas station, and Barbara Hepworth's on the beach. However, the last thing that I would claim is that they are all the same. Indeed, each of these is different, and, one might surmise, have to do with brain function of either a healthy or unhealthy brain. The descriptions suggest a change in consciousness, a deepening of conscious awareness which brings with it a boundless living in the moment which is arrested with the restoration of language. The boundlessness experience seems to turn on intuitive awareness, a phenomenological feeling of *what this moment is like* given the absence of language, and possibly, the momentary collapse of ontological categories. This, I believe, is the collapse of the subject/object distinction, as an experiential mode to which I referred in Chapter 1.

Note that this collapse is short-lived for without the subject/object distinction, we would live in chaos. As humans, we *live* subject and object. We cannot escape this. The idea that we constitute the world as we live requires that there be something other than our consciousnesses to be constituted. Yet from the perspectives of physics, biology, and our pure physicality, we are one with the world. These factors, however, do not erase subject and object because we are dealing with different ideas. We do not experience the world of physics for example. We experience the *effects* of the sub-atomic world, just as we experience the effects of our biology. In neither case do we experience, for example, the exchange of gases, the working of the micro-biome, the way in which we hang together.

We need, therefore, to distinguish amongst various experiences: of what, by what and the purpose or function of various experiences. I argued earlier for a primitive notion of self as an effect and as a constituted entity. 'Self' is phenomenological, an experiencing consciousness in an ontologically independent world but on which self is dependent (ontologically and phenomenologically). The world retains its integrity: the world makes me, I do not make it. As subjects, we constitute ourselves as objects. The self is the object of the I. In this sense, the self is a kind of fictional construction which is the effect of the turn to what is going on in our consciousnesses, that is, when we become aware that we are thinking/feeling/emoting. In other words, this is the rise of self-referentiality. Self is an intentional object, something about which we think. The self is a way of thinking about the I that each of us is. When we think about ourselves, we cannot think about the I that we each are, as it thinks, for that would be like trying to look at our consciousnesses. Furthermore, as a broad ontological point, I hold that there can be no I if there is no other, and its converse, that there can be no other if there is no I (I *iff* other).[1]

On one level, 'I *iff* other' has to do with language use: we learn about I, myself, self, and things apart from what is, basically, self-consciousness. We establish I and other through our experience, but we name them as we learn the languages we are taught. This does not mean, however, that I *iff* other does not hold. Rather, it suggests that the learning of a language and how to use it gives us a conceptual framework on which to build ourselves in the world. Language and ontology are, then, intertwined in this instance.

The original experiences each of us has prior to our practising the language we learn (and that is important, for practise make language use concrete) are the building blocks for I *iff* other. We reach for the breast (basic instinct), grip the fingers held out to us, cry when we are uncomfortable and learn to play and respond to what is other than ourselves, and we do this without language even when words might be being spoken to us (and that is a primary part of the language learning).

Subject and object become embedded in each other as we learn. That is our everyday experience of the world.

This does not mean that we did not experience the world prior to our learning language. What it suggests is that with different circumstances, we experience differently. Experience or the idea of what happens to or for us is not simple. Some of what we experience we *can* capture in language; some of it we cannot. When we are not yet language users, we cannot capture our experiences with words. Where we are language users, our consciousnesses are such that language awareness can be 'turned off' as was the case with Annie Dillard. Yet even then, we have access through memory, to the language in which we can subsequently describe a wordless experience. This means that we can recall in language what has happened to us, outside language. This is what has happened in the cases about which I've been talking; but critically, it also means that we can operate *outside* the subject/object distinction.

What follows from this is that there is a mode of conscious awareness not expressed in the subject and object distinction. Conscious awareness can become a pure, sensuous, experience, with no boundaries: in such cases, the subject/object distinction has collapsed. And this is what Annie Dillard alludes to when language returns and ruptures her pure experience. Note that this is not a regular, 'normal' state of affairs. Hence we cannot make a totalising claim about what is and what is not the case *tout court.* On this basis, the given-ness of subject and object through language and then the silencing of language and the disappearance of that distinctive given-ness constitute the possibility and actuality of self-awareness, of the I and self.[2]

Because of the ongoing changeableness of our consciousnesses, when we experience ourselves we are experiencing *something* even when we are changing and even if that something does not exist as a stable, unchanging entity. Indeed what we experience does not have to exist, in order for us to experience it. As a general rule, sometimes what we experience does indeed exist, even if it is unstable, changing and impermanent (people, rocks, trees, rainbows, hunger); sometimes what we experience does not (the characters in a story, angels, divine beings). That we are phenomenological selves, who feel and know what it is like to feel, with memory and who are agents in the world with consequences for our actions, is important morally.

Hence there is an on-going something which we are *experientially, phenomenologically* and morally: this is our consciousness. But consciousness is different from both self and I: consciousness is the means by which we are able to constitute ourselves as subjects and as objects. Even when we are meditating, say, in mindfulness practice, there is basic *awareness of* the fluctuations of the mind. It is that basic awareness which we are, a phenomenological experiencing of ourselves without words, without naming and categorising.[3] In that sense, meditational practices in which I and self are absent, is very like what I am talking about in the collapse of the subject and object distinction. Consciousness is our neurological foundation that, phenomenologically, makes us what we are and provides the basis for our moral actions and lives. Language is what delivers us to our I and our self. We can still experience without language, and that is what happens in epiphanic moments. We now come back to change and foundations.

So Back to Change

Change: we all know that change in human lives is ubiquitous: material, psychological, spiritual changes, map our ways through the world, map our lives. Some of the changes we experience are intentional, some unintentional and accidental, some unavoidable and predictable. We change ourselves through, and are changed by mere living, and we also change or affect the worlds in which we live. So we are all familiar with change and with different sorts of changes with different properties or qualities and we all know that both the cause and the effects of change are multiple. Nature, Beauty, and Art are thus joined by a fourth member, change, to form a quartet which grounds us existentially. And what they ground are our living bodies and psyches.

Yet the idea of the perfection of the unchanging as the ultimate reality has permeated much of our thinking for thousands of years. In the Western tradition, two obvious examples of this are the idea of an immutable, all powerful, all-knowing, God, on the one hand, and on the other, the human self, the personal soul which survives after death and will, eternally, either, enjoy heaven with the Divine or suffer hell with the Devil. In Indian philosophies, *purusha*, *atman*, *Brahma*, and rebirth attest to a belief in an unchanging ultimate reality.

Although the association between the personal (the self) and the impersonal or objective (God, the divine, *Brahma*) seems evident, the association is illusory. I say this for two reasons. We can never know for certain that there is an unchanging divine, what 'ultimate reality' is, or if the very notion is actually fully comprehensible (and physics and mathematics in the twentieth and twenty-first centuries suggest otherwise). And secondly, surviving death, presumably as the being one is (and has become?) when one dies, is problematic. Given that we cease to exist as living bodies and that the findings of neuroscience suggest a necessary relationship between a functioning brain and a living consciousness, there are good reasons for doubting conscious survival after death.[4]

The question, 'How does one account for 'change' within these philosophies?' yields a network of puzzles. As well as those I have just suggested, we can wonder about what is the relationship between immutability (un-change) and mutability (change). Is it structural, formal, substantial? Does immutability generate mutability, and if so, how? What is it that changes and what is it that remains unchanged? How can moral improvement be accounted for even in terms of sacramental forgiveness, say? In theology, if humans are made in the image of God and God is unchanging, how can humans change? If there are two substances, material and immaterial that make up what each of us is, what is it that brings them together? For it seems to be difficult to proceed without postulating the existence of different substances, as in Western thinking, spiritual/mental and physical/material, or as in Indian Samkhya, *purusha* and *prakriti*.

In our changing lives, we ask questions such as these and we develop ideas, sentiments, theories, and some of us learn about experimental physics and our origin in the stars as we grow into maturity. All of this comes to us through two avenues: innate capacities, and our experience which is the experience of an individual consciousness in the world, in a community. All of what is written is story-telling, not necessarily fictional, from an individual or collective perspective, informed by simple life itself, sometimes by scientific experiment, sometimes by Art practice, by business arrangements, by theorising, and always by birth and death. These are instances of the fabric of being for us, for the human adults into whom we grow. We do, and are, many of these dimensions of human being from the time we are born. We are nourished and played with and guided into childhood through recognition, most often by the recognition of our mothers.[5]

Hence our everyday experience of life from birth to death is not only enveloped by change, within change, resulting in even further change, but *is* change. And change is not simply a personal matter. Consider seasons, day and night, drought and flood, gentle lapping waves upon the shore and tsunami, political peace and upheaval. Each of these cases shows us that we live in a constantly changing environment, an environment external to us, and mostly beyond our control. In all of this, we can, and this is a paradox, on-goingly recognise something of ourselves that seems to be unchanging! I might have a different body from the one that I had at ten years old and experience the change in the seasons, but there seems to be a constant consciousness of 'I' or 'me' and 'my' which I nonetheless recognise it as my own. I have learned that ageing is an intrinsic part of my life, that ageing brings change and there is a way in which I have grown with my body and this is always situated in the natural world of seasonal change. But, and here we go on a question relevant to my Introduction, what is the 'I', the 'me', and 'my' that seem to persist through these changes, the one that is wordless in an experience and then the creator of a running narrative? Does that 'I' change? And what is it about me that is changed in a transformative moment? Do we need a dualistic metaphysic to explain what is going on here? Let us think this through in another way.

We seem to think of human beings in paired, exclusive opposites: the material or physical, and the psychological or mental, subject or object. How these paired opposites are related to each other has been the concern of metaphysicians, cognitive scientists, theologians, and phenomenologists for a very long time. To varying degrees, the context of such concerns and research has been taken into consideration, or not.

We can see from this that human lives are in flux no matter what. We seek change deliberately to find food and water, to reclaim land and restore basic needs and symbolic histories. In the Western world, we can begin exercise programmes, take up yoga or painting, begin to meditate, begin running or swimming, start a new job, write a poem, give birth, or make a new recipe. Our wealth and self-centred philosophies allow us to do this. But as well as physical effects, these body-oriented activities have an effect on our psyches. Change is what we want when we are lucky enough to be able to seek psychological help. We might decide, or be forced to admit that it's time to deal with trauma, to relieve ourselves of obsessive thoughts, to stop feeling depressed, to get out of an unhappy relationship, to deal with old, disturbing, memories, to understand a dream. This urge to do things differently implies that we want to move to a different psychological place.

Psychological transformation affects political action (and vice-versa) when we protest, vote, speak out against tyranny, escape to a better life: change here is envisaged as emancipatory. For we also seek change because we are in communities that matter to us, and we, to them. Marcus Aurelius noted that

> You must care for the salvation of all human beings, and serve the human community. Nature has fixed as a principle that your particular usefulness should be the common usefulness; and, reciprocally, that the common usefulness should be you particular usefulness ... You must remember that there is a community between human beings, which has been formed by Nature herself.
>
> *cited in Hadot, 1995: 192*

It is not merely our minds involved in these contingencies however: we exercise our bodies, we eat with our bodies, we fast, we suffer, we love, we give birth, and we die. Mind and body work together in the hope of bringing about change that is beneficial, that will bring happiness and a sense of well-being, even if death is the ultimate end. It is not mind alone however, but the pivotal role played by consciousness in the conjunction of mind and body in fact and through awareness in consciousness. The various plays of touch (sound, smell, new vista) are intrinsic to these experiences and processes, whether pre-conscious or fully aware in consciousness.

We experience on many different levels and in different ways, in our minds and in our bodies, depending on mental and emotional disposition, on biology, and also on sociocultural, geographical, and historical contingencies and contexts. This range of possible experiences leads, though, to a further question: just what is experience?[6] When we observe new-born babies, we can see that they experience: they nuzzle for the nipple, they cry when they are uncomfortable, they begin to smile in response to encouragement from their carers (mostly mothers). Indeed, studies show that babies respond to the maternal voice *in utero*, as well as to music, and these studies suggest that new-borns have already developed memory (Lang et al., 2020; Särkämö et al., 2013). As foetuses and as babies we respond to a world that comes to us, through sound, sight, touch, smell, taste. The world does not come as a whole. Indeed the world comes to us in singularity, in bits and pieces: in the voice heard, in the nipple that satisfies, in the smile that we learn is just ours, in the bright toy that catches our attention.[7] But we learn that these elements of our experience are part of a larger context: the breast and the smile belong together, and the bright toy appears with the bearer of breasts and smile. Our bodies synthesise, bring things together, and we are unaware of these early stages of the primitive, early experience that becomes us, even if we do not recall any *in utero* experience. Babies are massive and complicated response organisms who begin to learn that they are individuals amongst other individuals *and in a world* even before they become speakers of a language. The point here is that experience is initially response/and unconscious memory formation, it is primitive, the stuff on which all else is built.[8]

Change Before Words....

Let me distinguish between the consciousness manifested by the body as a living organism that needs to adapt to its environment; and the consciousness that is the living subject. My body is aware of what is happening to it, even before the existence of me. I learn to be a me, a reflective, conscious being. I exist only when I can respond consciously, deliberately, that is to say intentionally. A distinction is, here, necessary. On the one hand, my body is a conscious organism without my knowing this to be the case even *before* I know it to be the case. Much as a foetus responds to its environment, so do all living things. Our bodies strive towards being (Spinoza & Gutmann, 1949 Book 3 Prop 6). We need to think of this striving as a form of consciousness in which a stimulating environment interacts with the receptive organism which it hosts. This is a kind of primitive pre-reflective consciousness.[9] It is a consciousness that is manifest across all living beings, a phenomenal consciousness perhaps because there is something that it is like for a creature to be what it is. Philip Goff captures some of my meaning in the following:

> There's something that it's like for a rabbit to be cold, or to be kicked, or to have a knife stuck in it. There's nothing that it's like in contrast, for a table to be cold, or to be kicked, or to have a knife stuck in it (or so we ordinarily suppose). There's nothing that it's like *from the inside*, as it were, to be a table. We mark this difference by saying that the rabbit but not the table is conscious ... In some sense a rabbit is aware of the world around it, but it is doubtful that it is able to think reflectively about itself as an occupant of that world. The lack of self-awareness does not bar the rabbit from enjoying a rich and inner experience. Thus the rabbit is conscious in the phenomenal sense.
>
> *Goff, 2017: 2*

'What it is like' from the inside is the basis of experience. However, it is a slippery notion, depending on the level and sophistication of consciousness. As I noted above, our bodies respond to our environment without our being aware that they are (because we have no notion of 'our' or 'my') so that there is a sense in which we experience, as bodies, in a way similar to the rabbit. Response tells us that there is something going on: shivering, escaping, feeling pain: fight and/or flight responses. But the point is that, as bodies we do not know, and are not even aware of such experience, because our brains kick in to protect us before we develop consciousness that tells us that *we* are aware. In the beginning, the living organism which is each of us does not register its awareness as its own, even though there is an *as if* response to what it's like from the inside. Language is needed to articulate this. The fight/flight response is evidence of consciousness, and evidence of experience, but not evidence of self-consciousness.

So what I am arguing is that the basis of experience is in the structures of the brain: primitive structures ground primitive consciousness. The body is aware, as a living being, but the primitive mind and self-consciousness experience changes from the response/reaction *in utero* as we age, and we mature and acquire language, and as our reflective consciousnesses develop. We do not remain primitive: we act upon the environment, just as it acts upon us. Part of that is flight/fight. As small babies, as children, we begin to understand ourselves as distinct entities who can act deliberately in our environments. What is more, we learn to think about ourselves *as* ourselves, and we learn that the environments in which we find ourselves are not always under our control, no matter how intentionally we act. That realisation reinforces ourselves as individuals, yet also reinforces the distinctness of the world, our environment, from ourselves. This is a *conscious* realisation; that is to say we begin to be aware that we are aware. Consciousness and awareness come together, always from the first: hunger, a pooey nappy and discomfort, pain, register themselves in our bodies and establish us as ourselves. But the nature of consciousness itself changes over time.

When we become aware that we are aware, for example, our experience changes and we move into a different mode of consciousness, one in which consciousness itself is capable of objectifying itself. Consciousness, awareness, and experience are the changing facets of the changing beings we become. I want, then, to run with this idea: there are two 'moments' of intentionality: what we might think of as naïve or primary, directed, intentionality outside of will and deliberation that is activity and can be thought of as *conatus*, our immersion in the world always, already from the start. This fundamental intentionality has to do with structural ability of consciousness and with a natural, biological turning towards the world, after the manner of enactivist theory and practice. 'Practice' here refers to what is actually happening to us, how we are in the world, what we are doing. On this account, primary intentionality is not about representation.[10] Rather, it is more to do with how consciousness and the mind work. As living creatures in the world, as part of Nature, we need to, and always do, find ourselves in this world. We do that through the way in which our brains work in consciousness and in the mind. We are directed towards where we are, initially for reasons of survival. We see this in the way a newly born baby nuzzles towards its mother's nipple and latches on.

The second moment of intentionality is to do with self-conscious awareness, of ourselves and our situation, our contexts. This can be thought of as secondary intentionality which frames an object towards which it deliberately sends itself. This does involve representation, where something can be re-presented to my consciousness. When I think of my favourite ice cream, I form an idea, deliberately, around that notion and perhaps even imagine myself eating it and what it feels and tastes like. I frame the object, make it specific, bring it into my consciousness as a mental presence. That I can do this depends on the primitive ability of my human mind to 'exit' itself, to employ its structure, towards the world.

Given this distinction, we might think of existential moments as consciousness states with an unintended intentional object, that is to say, in terms of the first moment of intentionality. *They are spontaneous.* We, as it were, *spontaneously* return to a basic functioning of consciousness. And that is, perhaps, wherein the uniqueness lies, considering that so much of what we do is subject both to narration and deliberate intention, framed by either personal preference or by social practice, and often, both. Many of our actions and activities are a result of habit, a product of having learned how and what to do in particular situations. In that sense, they can be unconscious but nonetheless deliberate as we draw on past experience and respond to the circumstances in which we find ourselves.

This is all very nice. Yet we surely cannot be happy with talking about enactivist cognitive science, or neuroscience, or experience or mindfulness, without taking seriously the point I just made about babies, newly born or not. For it seems to me that theorists rarely, if ever, take into account the fact that all human beings are born (and die). Natality, as Hannah Arendt has argued, is the condition of all humanity, indeed the condition for anything human.[11] We are in this world, in Nature, because of our birth. We do not come into the world fully formed and begin thinking when we are adults. Nor are we thrown into the world as Martin Heidegger said, in all seriousness, trope or not. Varela, Thompson, and Rosch seem to think this an appropriate turn of phrase (Varela et al., 1991: 113). We are squeezed and pushed and sometimes pulled into the world, rather than thrown ('Thrown by whom?' one wonders). The almost aggressive connotation of 'thrown' suggests a limited understanding of both pregnancy and birth; and it also overlooks the tenderness and care with which most children are surrounded as they grow.

It is during this period of learning and inquiring, that we begin to become familiar with our worlds, our cultures, and ideologies to which we are submitted. They are given as that with which we work, and as that which makes us. Denial or forgetfulness or ignorance of our natality repudiates our emergence into a pre-formed world, one that pre-exists us. In that sense, again contrary to Varela, Thompson, and Rosch, the world is pre-given. They assume, along with Marvin Minsky whom they cite in their discussion of 'Cartesian anxiety',[12] that the notion of a pre-given world implies its full independence.[13] In my view the world is pre-given but not phenomenologically independent of a perceiver. Its ontological independence and integrity must be a given, however.

Theorising without taking this into account, even with the added option of talking about practical implications or settings, or arguing for a radical groundlessness, misses the point of origins, of our embodiment, of our very existence. It misses that we are in and of Nature.

In all of this, our consciousnesses are affected through our senses, through both conscious and what either is, or becomes, unconscious experience. Unconscious experience nevertheless assumes the first moment of intentionality, of the body's striving towards being. Conscious experience drives us towards self-consciousness as we become aware of happenings around us, things that we might have caused and things which affect us, and, well, things that are just there: traffic, sunsets, rainbows, accidents, loud noises from building sites. And it is to that that we learn to attach language. All of our experience occurs because we are *physically* (bodily) immersed in whole systems: the Natural world, and the social world of language and of practice, attitudes and values, secular or religious. Fundamentally, when we experience and when we change, *something happens in our brains*, in other words, *in our bodies*, either with or without conscious awareness. On this score, our consciousnesses are deeply related to the activities of our brains.[14] That is the great insight from science over the past 40 years: we are living, fleshy bodies and any change we experience is a bodily event involving our blood, our hormones, and our nerves. We know that these are parts and structures of our functioning anatomy and physiology; our consciousnesses and our self-conscious awareness are, indeed, part of our functioning anatomy and physiology. And research shows that consciousness exists throughout our bodies (Colombetti, 2014; Koch, 2012, 2019; Merleau-Ponty, 2002; Nagel, 2012; Noë, 2016; Pallasmaa, 2011, 2018; Varela et al., 1991; Zahavi, 2018). It does not show, though, that consciousness is reducible to our bodies (specifically our brains).

Yet self-conscious awareness seems to 'locate' ourselves in our brains, almost as if we are separate and separable from both our bodies which can become objects to us, and the world, our environment—Nature and human built—beyond our consciousnesses but of which we are aware. Here is where pronoun-use becomes slippery. My 'I' is different from your 'I'. And our 'we' may be different from another 'we'. And, then all of us, together, we humans, might construct an 'us' with an ontological integrity that is not well grounded. For the 'non-us', the Other (that is to say, human beings who are not ourselves), the object, what we observe, note, and experience), might become secondary to specific, individual or group human experience, even when we might know that without any Other, there is no us, indeed no I.[15] We seem to know what we are like and what the world is like, and what it is like to experience both. That said, object and experience of object are so closely intertwined, that it can be difficult to separate them, which is why what something feels like is necessarily bi-relational.

At the same time, what we experience has its own qualities, and this speaks to Zahavi's point above, in my 'Introduction'. My tactile experience and my knowledge of how things are, tell me that there is a boundary between the refrigerator and myself. So that even if there is difficulty in separating feeling from felt, experience from experienced (and precisely what we are experiencing) we generally live with both together; but we live *as if* there are boundaries between us as sensing subject, and what we sense. John Russon refers to this as 'the paradoxical co-happening of two intertwined infinites: the infinite context of subjectivity, "I," and the infinite "outside" reality, It' (Russon, 2017: 30). This fusion of infinites is separated by phenomenological boundaries that are not fictitious. We depend on a working notion of 'boundary' that is based not only on experience, but on what the world is like. For example, our skin is a boundary because it is, like all skin we can find in the world, that which ensures our physical integrity. Our recognising that the skin is a surface through which we interact with that which is on the 'other side' of, or outside the skin, is necessary for our survival. Likewise, most of us have a sense of privacy which is both assumed and insured not only by our skins as boundaries, but by the operations of our brains, what is *inside* our skulls. Yet the skin itself, the brain, and the skull are sustained by the environment: the air that we breathe, the nourishment we take, the protective measures we take to look after ourselves. Indeed the whole of the human body is both boundary and doorway to the world, and to itself. The world is what brings us to our senses, and establishes, right from the start, our inter-relationships with our environment. But the body cannot do that without functioning properly as a whole system. We are woven into the fabric of being and life simply because we exist.

Through this paradoxicality, the subject is created. Something happens in the brain that registers as *my experience* and as *your/our experience*. We use these pronouns to differentiate the self from the Other. Yet what something feels like is subject dependent, at least superficially. This pronoun-use fabricates a troublesome cleft in our ways of seeing the world. For we can begin to believe that we are distinct from, rather than part of, either our bodies or the environment, and that at bottom, all of our consciousness, our actions and intentions are individual.[16] Consciousness, in its very activity, in its ability to move among, above and below, around itself both unites and distinguishes. So although we are apparently psychologically distinct from Other, our ontological companionship with the world means that we have a kind of dependence that can be difficult to grasp. Too often, we seem to believe that the abstraction made possible by our consciousnesses—by the fact that we construe ourselves as subjects who observe, note, experience the what we behold—is so fundamental that is it more important than the world around us. The joyful union of parent with child gives lie to this conception.

Some of the change we experience involves not just a recognition, but a realisation that things are not as they once were, just a few seconds, a few minutes or hours or days or even longer. We become *transformed* through such change; that is to say, we are substantially altered, deep down, bodily, mentally, or psychologically so that we see ourselves, and are perhaps seen by others, as different from before. Such difference is phenomenological: it involves feeling, and the experience of realising that difference. Realising is an activity of consciousness, an act of awareness which brings us to ourselves in myriad ways. We move psychologically, through conscious awareness and through feeling.

But it is not all such an illuminating picture. Change and transformation occur as a result of trauma, pain, suffering. Again, deep, substantial alteration of human being through effect on the brain, indeed the whole organism, obscures hope, obscures optimism, destroys trust (van der Kolk, 2015). Such transformation is seen in colonial practices such as invasion and theft of land and power with a requisite denial of the humanity of original inhabitants, genocide, anti-Semitism, sexism, racism, classism (Brison, 2002; Grant, 2019; van der Kolk, 2015). Tenderness and compassion are salve, but barely redemptive, in these cases. We do not all live in happy worlds that encourage human flourishing and where all we have to worry about is whether to become vegan or stop eating gluten or whether our yoga tights are environmentally friendly. People starve, have inadequate housing and water, are caught in wars and are incarcerated and tortured, are inadequately clothed for their environment. That is to say, human experience ranges over pleasure, pain, suffering as well as illuminating, up-lifting moments.

In all of this, consciousness is central. As well as telling us about our experience, our consciousnesses *is* our awareness, make us aware of what something feels like, heightening our perception. 'What something feels like', involving only our bodies (pain, orgasm, itch, taste) or the world at large: a sunset, a thunderstorm, bird song, stars, sculpture, animal, the taste of a raspberry, a concert performance, an emotive word, the touch of velvet, the garden after rain, is self—and other-aware experience, sometimes separately, and sometimes, simultaneously. We feel *because* we are conscious bodies, bodies with flesh and bones, with nervous and sensing systems, and because we are inter-relational. We can never stand either existentially or ontologically aloof from the world and all of its features, be they Natural or human made in spite of our best efforts.

And to reiterate, our bodies are *in* and *of* the world: we are human animals who live in Nature, in ecological environments, the Natural world, the ecosphere, and we also live in human-made environments populated by human-made things. Yet what we are surrounded by is either the Natural world or derived from the Natural environment, transformed as it might be beyond what is understood as the Natural world. Transformation of Nature into human products involves touching and being touched by what the world feels like and by our reasoning and learning.

Now this is the thing: we are non-exclusive agents of changing Nature: Nature changes itself through us, and also quite apart from what we might want or plan. Storms, floods, earthquakes are all beyond our wills and control. The human propensity to inaugurate change is not always constructive and we see this in the warming of the planet and the destruction this brings: bushfires and even floods can be traced back to human activities; the decline in species diversity is definitely so.

So while I am talking about existential moments that are truly, wondrously transformative and involve the existential triad Nature, Beauty, and Art, there is also a down-side to this. It is terror and loss in which we are architects of our futures. While then, I am proposing that an existential experience is one in which our brains, our beliefs, and our sociocultural contexts are manifested in particular ways to bring us to an epiphany, we can be overcome by Nature in not so beautiful and artistic ways. But sometimes change that is insightful, expansive, and perhaps unpredictable happens, and we can learn to understand that when we attend to research from neuroscience.

And Beauty....

Many or even all of us have relationships with Beauty, Art, and with Nature that make life not merely bearable, but worth living and thoroughly happy. The sort of personal happiness that comes to us through them might be transitory, but the effect of that happiness can extend beyond the personal 'I' or self, into our social lives and communities and affect our human flourishing.[17] Beauty, Art, and Nature are so tied up in the fabric of our lives that were we never to experience them, we would be miserable, confined to Dante's Inferno. Art, Beauty, and Nature form a kind of existential triad that inspires, nourishes, and fills us with wonder, awe, and, sometimes, enlightenment. Art, Beauty, and Nature not only make us flourish, but protect us from the wolf of hate (Hanson, 2009).

By 'Beauty' I understand (and this is not a definition) the existence in an object, or of an arrangement of parts, such that a special kind of happy feeling is evoked that has to do directly with the object. What I mean by 'special kind of happy feeling' is that one in which we are transformed in a positive and uplifting way for having been in the presence of the object. We simply feel better. What is more, 'Art' is understood as the expression and articulation of relationships that we have to both the Natural and engineered or built environments in which we live. Hence the term 'Art' connotes visual, auditory and literal representations and imaginative re-figuring of the contexts in which we find ourselves. While we may not, ourselves, be makers of Art, our presence to Art occurs formally in galleries, churches, museums, and perhaps even our personal space where we live; and which are sometimes beautiful. Our presence to Art occurs each time we enter a built environment; how we enter that environment is crucial here. The means by which we enter, for example, by car or bus or aeroplane or boat or bicycle brings us immediately into a technological milieu that we take for granted and is yet an expression of human intercourse with the natural environment. That expression is artistic expression for design is paramount in the attempt to ease ourselves into the environment. Technology is Art par excellence.

Our relationship with Beauty, Art, and Nature is changeable, and flexible. It might be the case that yet another gallery or church or architectural masterpiece is one too many, and we can glaze over, as if we've had too much to eat or drink. Sometimes, we long for a crowded city street, with its landscape of busy bodies and traffic, and do not care for the fresh greenness or dry magnificence of a forest or desert. We flex and bend with our moods and contexts: our flexibility reflects the fact that we are constantly changing, a little or a lot.

Sometimes, we become aware that something has happened for which we can offer no account: we do not really know what, exactly, has transpired and we feel differently from before, perhaps elated or enriched psychologically in some way. What we do know, and this comes after as a kind of revelation, is that something is different from before as we turn in an altered way back into our own conscious awareness of self. In a sense, the self is momentarily suspended but consciousness persists and there is a before and an after with which we then reconnect. Nature, Beauty, and Art are responsible, sometimes, for this change. They have a felt presence in the psychologies of Sigmund Freud and Carl Jung. And in the philosophies of human flourishing. I turn, now to these.

Notes

1 For a full discussion of an argument to this effect, see my unpublished MA Thesis, held at ANU (Gray, 1990). I am not sure that I now agree with the whole details of this thesis, but, broadly speaking, I do still hold that the subject 'I' and the object, 'Self' are distinct.

This is the argument I develop, which has its origins in the transcendental philosophy of Immanuel Kant, and in the later work of Franz Brentano and Edmund Husserl:

1. consciousness is consciousness-of.
2. consciousness-of consciousness yields 'I'.
3. 'I' *simpliciter* is empty, a bare (naked) subject which intuits its own being.
4. intuiting its own being,'I' constitutes an object (Self) to untold or to know that being.
5. the object (Self) that is constituted by 'I' is an intentional object.*p. 49*

2 When Francisco Varela, Evan Thompson, and Eleanor Rosch use Tsultrim Gyamatso's *Progressive Stages of Meditation on Emptiness* and the *Abhidharma* to explore what the self is, they work with one of Gyamatso's assumptions, that 'the self has to be lasting … single … independent'. The argument seems to involve the idea of grasping: the self that we seek is the result of our grasping after something on-going, separate, independent, and they compare this with David Hume's futile attempt to find his self (although he asks what impression would give rise to such an idea) (Hume, 1975; Varela et al., 2016). We might assume these properties of the self, but, I suggest, that is by convention, and by our unacknowledged assumptions about the reality of an unchanging world subtending the world we experience. Yes, what we take to be ourselves *is* always changing. That does not mean that either self or I do not exist. There's a metaphysical assumption operating here, that there needs to be something stable and persisting in order for something to exist, a point which I am not going to argue here.

3 I do not think that this is addressed in Buddhist philosophy.

4 For conscious survival must surely be the case or else there is no substance to the claim that we live on, somehow, after death.

5 I've often wondered if in the bulk of their theorising, and discovery in and about the world, men even consider the fact that each of them is born from the body of a woman and that they have grown to be the persons they are. What Plato and Aquinas and David Hume and A.J. Ayer and Carl Jung and Sigmund Freud and Martin Heidegger and Daniel Dennett and John Russon and Carlo Rovelli and anyone else you care to think of and either mention or not, have in common, is their natality, their formation in the body of a woman; and predominantly, their growth in the care of a woman or women, mother or not.

6 For a full examination of human experience and also its relation to interpretation, see *Human Experience* (Russon, 2003) and *Sites of Exposure* (Russon, 2017).

7 John Russon's claim that '(t)he interpretation that constitutes experience is not a two-stage act of first receiving an uninterpreted object, and then overlaying it with an interpretation; rather it is only as already interpreted that it is there for me as a phenomenon. There are no raw data awaiting organization by a subsequent act. In experience, I directly perceive the object as a unitary, already meaningful phenomenon' (Russon, 2003) does not countenance primitive experience or the way in which we learn to interpret or how the brain synthesises. His view does not seem to accommodate infancy and childhood and the development of self-concept over time. Does one interpret from the beginning or does one learn to interpret over time? Is one's first experience an interpretation? Does a baby interpret that its nappy is wet or that it is hungry?

8 See Martha Nussbaum's comments on the defects of Stoic philosophy with respect to developmental psychology (Nussbaum, 2013: Introduction 2009: xiii).

9 Shaun Gallagher and Dan Zahavi describe the phenomenological distinction between pre-reflective and reflective consciousness thus:

> For phenomenologists, the immediate and first-personal givenness of experience is accounted for in terms of a pre-reflective self-consciousness. In the most basic sense

> of the term, self-consciousness is not something that comes about the moment one attentively inspects or reflectively introspects one's experiences, or recognizes one's specular image in the mirror, or refers to oneself with the use of the first-person pronoun, or constructs a self-narrative. Rather, these different kinds of self-consciousness are to be distinguished from the pre-reflective self-consciousness which is present whenever I am living through or undergoing an experience, e.g., whenever I am consciously perceiving the world, remembering a past event, imagining a future event, thinking an occurrent thought, or feeling sad or happy, thirsty or in pain, and so forth.
>
> *Gallagher and Zahavi, 2021*

In my view, we can consciously perceive the world without being aware that we are doing so, and this is the primitive pre-reflective consciousness to which I am alluding, and, perhaps, that to which they are referring.

10 Some recent theorists associate intentionality with representation. For a good summary of these views see Jacob (2019).

11 For a discussion of this point see Gray (2016).

12

> Either we have a fixed and stable foundation for knowledge, a point where knowledge starts, is grounded, and rests, or we cannot escape some sort of darkness, chaos and confusion. Either there is an absolute ground or foundation, or everything falls apart.
>
> *Varela et al., 1991: 140*

13 I acknowledge that Varela, Thompson, and Rosch refer to birth in their discussion of Tibetan Buddhism. For them, the Buddhist concept of birth, one of the 12 links (*nidana*) in the Wheel of Life suggests that birth (*jati*) is a moment at which 'one senses the causal chain and wants to do something about it' (Varela et al., 1991: 114). The idea that from birth one can sense that the causal chain is embedded in the idea of death and rebirth, *Samsara*, which is what they seem to be arguing, is contrary to human experience. Who remembers their birth or baby thoughts? According to Buddhist thinking, one retains memory from previous lives (although, as they are at pains to point out a foundational self does not exist: what retains memory or, indeed succeeds into a next life from this one?). The realising consciousness, the consciousness born and reborn with the ability to achieve *Sunyata* or emptiness of form and substantiality appears to me to embrace, rather than refute what might be thought of as existential foundationalism.

14 How the brain and consciousness are related is subject of debate amongst philosophers and neuroscientists. See, for example, Chalmers (2018), Colombetti (2014), Damasio (1994), Dennett (1992), and Thompson and Varela (2001).

15 I've argued this fully in Gray (2013, 2016).

16 For an interesting discussion of I- and we-intentions, see (Zahavi, 2015).

17 Martha Nussbaum uses the term 'human flourishing' as a translation of the Greek *eudaimonia* (Nussbaum, 2001) which is often translated as 'happiness' and I follow suit.

3

TOUCH, BEAUTY, PLACE

Beauty and the Beautiful[1]

I have chosen some well-known Plato texts to begin my fuller discussion of the idea of Beauty. Subsequent theorising of 'Beauty' owes much to these early discussions, whether as elaboration or as refutation. Firstly, the idea that Beauty is something beyond an individual case ('it' is a universal), and secondly, the idea that the attribution of Beauty might involve some one thing, which everything that is beautiful is held to possess, are introduced to us. Thirdly, the idea that Beauty is in the 'thing' beheld, and that Beauty is not dependent upon an observer, that it is beyond appearances, emerges. Relatedly, in being beyond appearances, Beauty is real, and in Plato's case, as also with Aristotle, Beauty is a Form, an absolute, an ideal. Elements of these themes have remained with us, apparent in debates over whether Beauty is objective or subjective, in ideas of perfection, harmony and balance, order, proportion and symmetry, and in controversies over love, pleasure, asceticism, and hedonism.[2] Let us explore this further.

We saw, earlier, in Nehamas' question and response, an example of a philosopher trying to figure out what Beauty is. He is treading a well-worn path, for it has been a long road. Nehamas begins with Plato, as many thinkers have done.[3] In *Greater Hippias* (Hippias Major), Socrates[4] asks Hippias to define '*kalon*' which is translated as both 'beauty' and 'fine'. For the purposes of this work, I shall refer to '*kalon*' as Beauty (Pappas, 2020). Socrates insists on asking, and then repeating his question: 'What is Beauty?' to the disquiet of Hippias whose answers Socrates refuses to endorse. Those answers include the proposal that Beauty is the appropriate and useful, answers which Socrates rejects because he is seeking a universal, Beauty in itself, evident in all that is beautiful. Further, Socrates is not simply looking for the *appearance* of Beauty. He wants to know what it is that makes a thing beautiful when it appears beautiful. He is not seeking individual cases of Beauty or the beautiful: he

DOI: 10.4324/9780429022975-4

wants essence—what it is that all individual things considered beautiful (like a maiden or a jug or a spoon) have that makes each of them beautiful (*The Collected Dialogues of Plato:* Greater Hippias, 1961).

Then again, in *Symposium*, Plato has Socrates recollecting a conversation with Diotima in which she maintains that 'love is of the beautiful'. Responses to Diotima's questions about desire in relation to beauty[5] and good and happiness lead to a discussion of acquisition or ownership of the thing desired. Later in that dialogue, Diotima distinguishes between corporeal Beauty and Beauty of the soul. She then argues for an ascending order of Beauty from Earthly things to absolute Beauty. She asks,

> But what if a man had eyes to see the true beauty – the divine beauty I mean, pure and clear, and unalloyed, not infected with the pollution of the flesh and all the colours and vanities of mortal life–thither looking, and holding converse with the true beauty simple and divine?

She asserts that such a vision would enable a man to have hold not of images, but realities. In this state one would 'become the friend of God and be immortal' (Plato et al., 1970). Diotima hypothesises a divine provenance in which realities—the True, the Forms, and the Form of all Forms—subsist, and of which the world of appearances, what we might think of as the mundane, is an imitation to varying degrees. This is, of course, a persistent theme in Plato's work.

We find a similar vision recounted in *Phaedrus*, in Socrates' debate with Phaedrus about erotic love, passion, and friendship.[6] Socrates claims that

> For the immortals, when they are at the end of their course, go forth and stand upon the outside of heaven; its revolution carries them round, and they behold the things beyond ... There abides the very being with which true knowledge is concerned; the colourless, formless, intangible essence, visible only to mind the pilot of the soul. The divine intelligence, being nurtured upon mind and pure knowledge, and the intelligence of every soul which is capable of receiving the food proper to it, rejoices at beholding reality once more, after so long a time, and gazing upon truth, is replenished and made glad, until the revolution of the world brings her round again to the same place. In the revolution she beholds justice, and temperance, and knowledge absolute, not that to which becoming belongs ... 'real knowledge really present where true being is'.
>
> *Plato, 1970: Phaedrus, 247b–e*

His evocation of the realm where true knowledge and being are, is not where most human beings find themselves. Even though the principle of life for human beings, is self-moving and animate, 'unbegotten and immortal' there is yet a problem with the human soul. As in the *Republic*, he characterises the soul as a chariot drawn by a pair of winged horses. In humans, one of the horses is a troublesome beast, 'so the management of the human chariot cannot but be a difficult and anxious task'. The thing is though, that the soul can work perfectly or imperfectly. The horse, the analogue of the soul, can damage or lose its wings, yet remain eager 'to behold the Plain of Truth'. For the 'pasturage found there, which is suited to the highest part of the soul' brings nourishment to the soul, enabling the wing to grow once more (Plato, 1970: Phaedrus, 246a–248d).

The soaring wing 'is most akin to the divine' and is what transports the soul to the realm of the gods. That is where it encounters the divine which is 'beauty, wisdom and goodness and the like'. When the soul fails to be fed by these wonders, but is, instead, nourished by evil and foulness, it fails to flourish. An encounter with the divine is what lies behind the madness of the lover, the one who sees the beauty of the Earth but 'is transported by the recollection of the true beauty' (Plato, 1970: Phaedrus, 249d–e). And this is the madness of love that 'is the greatest of heaven's blessings' (Plato, 1970: Phaedrus, 245b–c).

So that is at least part of Plato's story. For me, it is seductive because it does provide an answer to the question of what makes beautiful things, beautiful; and also because Plato has come up with a pretty good mythological narrative. But I am also persuaded by Plato's association between justice, goodness, knowledge, truth, and Beauty. We do think of these qualities or virtues or graces as belonging to a family of desiderata, and to which many of us aspire. The question, however, is whether or not these *are* ideal Forms, the very being of everything in a domain beyond the alleged appearance of this Earth on which we all live. There is also the question about who has access to this splendid vision.

Plato asserts that

> every soul of man has in the way of nature beheld true being; this was the condition of her passing into the form of man. But all souls do not easily recall things of the other world; they may have seen them for a short time only, or they may have been unfortunate in their earthly lot, and, having had their hearts turned to unrighteousness through some corrupting influence, they may have lost the memory of the holy things they once saw.
>
> *Plato, 1970: Phaedrus, 249b–c*

The soul capable of seeing the truth, then, is this man, the one who recollects once more, following God and gazing upon true being. In Plato's view, the philosopher is the principal candidate for this (sorry, everyone else!).

Maybe the gods can enjoy the realm of perfection, of the real; and maybe philosophers can also aim to, and possibly achieve this vision. His conception of the Forms seems to apply to almost everything: that something is what it is, universally, because there is a quality or property that each individual thing has that it shares with every other thing that has the same property or agglomeration of properties. Yet the arguments advanced against this understanding are themselves persuasive, as Parmenides had argued earlier (Rickless, 2020). For example, if everything we encounter here on Earth is an imitation of what is real, what is the relationship between the copy and the real? If the copies participate, then what is the nature of the participation? Is the soul distinct from the body, ontologically, as Plato argues? Are we, as souls, re-incarnated into different bodies and maybe lucky enough to end up as philosophers? What, then, is the relationship between soul and body, between the gods and humans?

I do not want to defend or reject Plato's views. It is clear to me that what he argues has been part of the bedrock, and remains influential, in discussions of Beauty. What I shall say, however, is that we arrive through this discussion back at Nehamas's question about the nature of Beauty. Perhaps one of the lessons from this Platonic exploration of Beauty, love, and friendship is that they do seem to have a kind of completeness or perfection about them. Beauty, love, and justice are clearly transformative for they lift one out of apparent ordinariness to extraordinariness. This is a point on which Plato is very strong. And it seems to be born out by some of the experiences about which I have been talking, the transformation of the everyday for both Dillard and Hepworth, and so many others—perhaps you, the reader.

Plato's omission of an Earthly dimension to truth, beauty, and the real is predictable given his metaphysics. His ontology of a human being is dualistic: the non-material soul and the flesh. To admit that the Earthly, mortal body is capable of experiencing the real, of seeing it, is simply not on. That's the business of the soul. What happens here on Earth in our everydayness results in mere opinion, for most of us have lost our initial vision of the real, as we saw above. He is scathing when he discusses what it means to know and its relations to the real (Plato, 1999, 2003; Plato & Cornford, 1970). Opinion is a shadow of, and may even be contrary to, the truth. The further one is from the truth, the further one is from the real, the essence of being; the further one is from 'the divine beauty I mean, pure and clear, and unalloyed, not infected with the pollution of the flesh and all the colours and vanities of mortal life—thither looking, and holding converse with the true beauty simple and divine' which we saw Diotima state interrogatively. The pollution of the flesh, the colours, and vanities of mortal life is the very realm of opinion, is where we interact with each other, where we grow and learn. And for Plato, truth does not exist here.

He says that clear perception of what they see by those who are enraptured by vision of the real do not understand what they see since 'there is no radiance in our earthly copies of justice or temperance or those other things which are precious to souls: they are seen through a glass dimly' (Plato, 1970: Phaedrus, 250a–b). One possibility, given this, is that existential moments are moment when the soul catches sight of its original vision. That, however, would require that we accept Plato's construction of the soul as a life force independent of the human body. We would then need to resolve the obvious issues around metaphysical dualism. And that is not my concern here as I pointed out at earlier.

How one would know that there is no radiance in our Earthly copies is a problem, and it is a problem which Plato does not address. Plato is sold on an ideal, but it is not an imaginable ideal precisely because it is beyond human conception.

That said, humans *do*, sometimes, catch a glimpse of a radiance that *is* imaginable only because someone has experienced and not simply imagined or represented to themselves the apparently impossible ideal. Nothing can be added to or subtracted from this moment, it is full, complete. Such an experience might happen because one is in a certain frame of mind, the right place at the right time; or such an experience might come out of the blue, a spontaneous happening, an epiphanic moment. These are two different scenarios which capture some of the elements of the work on peak and optimal experiences, and also eureka moments.

A Walk Along the River

Perhaps emotion might have something to do with our response to and apprehension of, Beauty? John Kounios and Mark Beeman maintain that '(e)motions influence how you think, and how you think can influence your emotions'. They explore the research of emotion alongside the work of cognitive psychologists who have attempted to figure out what is going on in creative thinking and insight. Most of the studies they explore are laboratory based. I am not sure how much can be extrapolated from a laboratory setting in which experiences are constructed or manufactured, to experiences had outside the laboratory. One of the claims they make is that positive mood 'broadens attention and enhances creative insight'. fMRI showed that areas of the brain were activated when insight was anticipated and this also was the case when for positive mood. Again, this is in a laboratory setting. What is found out might be illuminating, but how spontaneity can be either created in a laboratory, or measured in the world, so to speak, is a problem. To argue from 'this is what is going on in a laboratory' to 'this is what is going on in the world of everyday experience' seems to me is a problematic form of inductive reasoning. That is why a collection of anecdotes is such an important research resource, perhaps the only one that really matters.[7] The question, 'does the firing of the brain cause us to have an insight, or does an insight cause the brain to fire in a particular way?' which echoes Kounios' and Beeman's claim that there is a reciprocal relationship between emotions and thinking, needs also to be asked here. If consciousness is more than brain processes, that is to say, irreducible to brain firings, pings and lightings-up of fMRI or EEG, that question is relevant. At the moment, the only way I see of solving this is to for whole populations to wear portable tracking equipment which records what their brains are doing when and where. This amounts to surveillance, a compliant population and a revision of both political and ethical thinking (think of *Minority Report*). Practical considerations are also pertinent. But let us not wander into the world of science fiction, and bring these conceptions of Beauty into our own lives.

The Prosaic and Beauty

Now I want you to consider the possibility that you are walking along the river with a friend. It is a calm, clear, soft, blue, warm morning. You say to you friend, or your friend to you, with a sweeping arm gesture, 'Isn't this beautiful!?' You are taken up by the magnificence of where you are. Your friend replies, 'Well it does nothing for me'. Your friend is not taken up by the magnificence you are experiencing. Perhaps you have, metaphorically speaking, walked to the rim of heaven as Martha Nussbaum puts it (Nussbaum, 2013: 17), but your friend has not? You have seen more, perhaps, your friend has seen less. You might be a soul that can recollect the origins whilst your friend is not. Whatever the case, something is going on for each of you that is quite different. You are physically in the same place, presumably your senses of sight are equally engaged. However, you both are *seeing* differently. This emerges in your response to your surroundings and her reply to you. Maybe she is having a bad hair day of the soul: she is cranky with someone, or slept badly or is hungry or is not feeling well or her shoes are hurting her or she is out of condition. You are experiencing none of these things. Instead, you are just ambling along, chatting away and looking at the trees, the cliff face, the sky, hearing the birds and smelling the air. Your friend is closed and you are open, you might think.

Well, we may never know what is going on for either of you. What we do know is that there is difference in experience, and difference in perception of the where-ness of you both. There is a *qualitative* difference. You are, it seems, differently disposed towards the world on that day. It may be the case that next time you walk together along the river, you are having a bad hair day of the soul or are sad that someone you knew has just died, and that she is the one who is ebullient and notices the things that you might have noticed had you been in a different frame of mind.

Go back to the river for a moment. You are in the bad place on this particular morning. Your friend is jauntily tripping along beside you, chatting away, laughing about some event that happened at work or a funny thing one of her children had said. You can hear what she is saying, and you understand that she is happy. You remain wrapped in the darkness of your soul. Suddenly, you see some black swans gliding down on to the river. They look magnificent and they land with a ripple, disturbing the water. But it is a beautiful ripple. Then they float effortlessly along on the water. Your friend has seen none of this, or if she has, she doesn't say so. You stop, gob-smacked, your darkness vanishes, and you are transfixed for a moment by Nature and Beauty. You instantly feel better. You grab your friend's arm and say, 'Wow! Did you see that?' Initially, your friend does not know what you are talking about; she has been so engaged in her own narrating world, that she is oblivious to the where-ness of you both. But then she sees, and you marvel together.

I am using these examples to point out that our psychological disposition affects how we see the place we are in, currently in. *How* we see affects *what* we see. Most of us probably realise this. Both of these are qualitative in so far as the how and what will vary depending on mood. From that, though, it does not follow that what you are seeing and experiencing is not real, nor is it real only to you. The alerting of your friend and her response testifies to this. This could mean, therefore, that seeing Beauty is dependent on mood and disposition, together with awareness. We might wonder about the importance of this dependency: does psychological dependency (for that is what it is) make the perception of Beauty a purely subjective matter? Is a tree reflected in a perfectly still, clear river, beautiful even if you are, or I am closed and grumpy, say? Are the eyes of the once beloved still beautiful even after love has disappeared?

The introduction of awareness *changes* what is going on. 'Awareness' is intentional, that is to say, awareness has an object and in these cases, the object of awareness (Nature). Here, the subject/object distinction is operating in a profound way. It is apparent that you are not in a solipsistic universe, for you are in the company of your friend (and let us not adopt the sceptic's view that you could be imagining the existence and presence of your friend as a result of brain injury or drugs or both). You are *both* walking along the river. There is an exchange between the two of you. You are both touched by the scene which you are inhabiting, enjoying, noticing. Your brains are configuring the where, the what, and the how in a particular way. But your brains do not manufacture what is going on. There is a causal relationship between you and place. Beauty has something to do with perception, but it also has to do with what the world (Nature) is like, how it affects your senses, and the place you are in. The ontological integrity of Nature is preserved in your apprehension of Beauty. Evidence for this claim comes from across many cultures, where sunsets, rainbows and finely woven fabric, the look in the eye of the beloved, and the Beauty of the divine, the touch of a feather and the warmth of sunshine or the coolness of snow, are found. If each of these is an occasion of Beauty, then we can surely attribute Beauty to something beyond human fabrication, just as we would justice and fairness, harmony, order, and balance. Plato's intuition that there is a reality shared by similar things, and that there is a perfect form of that reality, seems plausible, from this perspective. But, as Aristotle later pointed out, the Forms do not have to be as Plato described.

But what does the evidence amount to? Perhaps because we are all physiologically similar in relevant ways that affect perception, we are bound to respond as we do? That is to say, relative to the nature of Nature and the nature of human physiological responses to stimuli, Beauty turns out to be directly related to the confluence of (at least) two relata: human consciousness and the Natural world. Beauty is not some one thing or group of things but it is created in an encounter. Mood, disposition, temperament can be factored in as well as change in time of day, weather, season. Beauty, on this account, is real, *it is there before our eyes or ears* but is multifaceted. Beauty is not simply in the eye of the beholder, but in the conjoint presence of the beholder and what is beheld.

So we have here, two different accounts of 'Beauty'. Are we any closer to figuring out what Beauty is? This I doubt, but what a wonderful problem with which to be concerned! The distinction between a something that is a possessor of Beauty, and the beholding subject, on one level, is not a strict division. Yet Nature has an ontological integrity beyond the human subject; the human subject and Nature are psychologically and epistemologically related. We are not the sum of the world. Disposition and awareness are elements in the experience of Beauty, and we shall come across this later in my discussion of Sigmund Freud and Carl Jung. For now, let us return to touch.

Back to the Theorists

Like Immanuel Kant, Umberto Eco points out that what is beautiful has been closely linked to what is good (Kant, 2012). Eco discusses the idea of the desirable and the beautiful and, echoing Plato, notes that a 'beautiful thing is something that would make us happy if it were ours, but remains beautiful even if it belongs to someone else' (Eco, 2004: 10). What is beautiful does not simply make us happy. Beauty helps us to flourish, to strive for what is good, to live what is good, and to bring goodness and beauty to all living things (as Buddhists would have it). So Beauty involves a kind of generosity that is intrinsic to flourishing.

If it is the case, as I claim, that Beauty always involves touch then whatever it is in a beautiful thing that makes us happy involves touch. As sentient beings, we are touched by many aspects of the world: our consciousnesses reach out into the world as the world reaches into us. The kind of reaching about which I am speaking involves reciprocity and exchange which draws us into networks of imaginings, activities, and change. And it is in this process of touching and reaching that we find Beauty in what we think of as beautiful things or experiences. We feel happy in virtue of being touched and being able to be touched. I also note that we feel saddened and distressed by something that causes us anguish or unhappiness or misery. Touch might be either benign or malignant or even neutral if we are not noticing what is going on around us. Even so, touch is in our bodies and the way in which we engage with and encounter the world.

In my extended use of 'touch' together with my claim that Beauty touches us, we might consider that competing theories of Beauty (Plato, Kant, Schopenhauer, Eco) are relevant at different moments. We might, for example, realise that when we are touched by Beauty, it is not always in the same way or by the same things. We respond to Beauty according to circumstances, to situation and context as I was arguing above. The feeling of frost under the feet and between the toes is exhilarating and transforms a freezing morning into an occasion of wonder at the Beauty of the natural world. Yet the appearance of a rainbow over a river on a cold winter day when one is safely snuggled by a warm fire delights precisely because one does not have one's toes in frost. The Beauty of an intensely coloured, fully formed rainbow hovering in the forefront of a deep grey background somehow transcends the coldness of the winter day, and transforms us. In either case, that there is something to which one responds is of extreme importance. Beauty is not fully in the eye of the beholder: what is beheld stimulates a special response, a response associated with ideas of Beauty, wonder, delight, pleasure, and happiness. … Eco's assertion that Beauty makes us happy is spot on.

We might note that in each of these moments of encounter with Beauty there is a tendency to reify: Beauty is seen as a thing. If that is the case 'Beauty' and 'the beautiful' are not seen as property, quality, or characteristic that is in, or an effect. And given this, one might argue as a way of resolving the conundrum of exactly what Beauty is, that there is no such thing as Beauty, only instances that are manifested in different ways across a range of occasions, objects, and situations. Without the world and without the senses, there would be no Beauty: Beauty, we might argue, is unlike the stars and Uluru at sunset which exist no matter what (assuming the existence of the cosmos as it currently is). Yet language use reinforces the tendency to reify: we speak not only of a beautiful sunrise or sunset, but, in English, we seem to easily slip into using this word as a noun. Witness Socrates' questions, 'What is Beauty?' and 'How do we define the beautiful?' (translated from Greek).

As I remarked in my Introduction, both Art and Beauty deal with relationships in and between characteristics of wholes and parts, and a subject capable of feeling happiness. So let us suppose, that there is no one characteristic, that we are not Platonists and that there is no 'realm' of intelligible Forms, that sits behind and beyond this world of appearances, and in which appearances consequently participate: let us imagine that the Platonic Form of Beauty is merely fanciful metaphysics. Such a view assumes something beyond because in spite of our best efforts, it seems as if we cannot, not really, explain the way in which we describe and experience the world, especially Beauty and figuring out what Art is. Well, we don't have to postulate that intelligible realm at all. But we can run with Aristotle's idea of universals, as derivative of the world around us. That is to say, we build up or create the idea or the notion of Beauty from the objects which we encounter in this world. The world is the source together with our responses as we inhabit the very domain to which we respond. Both Art and Beauty are, to some extent, relational. This will mean that there is a way of understanding 'Beauty' which is contextual, but which is not totally subjective, and which is generalisable across a number of different objects and occasions and which does not reify Beauty apart from its instantiations. On this rendering, it is possible that context is not tied to a specific space and time: that is to say, that there are other contexts which would manifest Beauty in the same way. 'Beauty', on this reading, becomes a property or a characteristics of situation and response and what there is in the world, and especially in the world of Nature.

Eco's idea that whatever is beautiful, is so, regardless of ownership evokes the idea of disinterest (Kant, 2007: 36). I cannot grasp or hold what is beautiful as if my ownership added something to its Beauty. To the contrary, ownership is quite irrelevant to the Beauty of whatever it is. Hence we might listen, as I did not so long ago, to Strauss' 'Four Last Songs', sung, say by Jessye Norman who sings them so wonderfully and had recently died; and we might weep. My weeping was a mixture of pleasure and delight, sadness and loss: the songs are full of tenderness, and magnificent musical emotion. To pick up Eco's point, I did not envisage ownership of either the music or the performance; there was a sense in which it was simply beautiful. The objects I encountered, Norman's voice, the music, the performance contained within them, something to which I responded. I recognised what seemed to me to be an intrinsic Beauty of this music and this voice. Furthermore, I believed that it was, and would remain beautiful even if I had not heard it and even though it was not mine. I was struck by something that came to me through the sound that reverberates across my ear drums, that was interpreted by my brain, that said to my consciousness: this is Beauty, this is beautiful! This is auditory touch in a specific and wonderful way.

Touch and Beauty

Touch and narrative go together. We hear, we read and it is sound and light coming to our bodies that create the possibility and actuality of narrative. Yet sound and light can come to us, unaccompanied by narrative, as Annie Dillard notes. Touch and Beauty also go together when our senses bring us to a special kind of awareness in which there is a direct connection between a sensed object and our consciousnesses. We hear beautiful melody and voice; see a beautiful sunrise; we hear beautiful bird calls; we taste beautiful ice cream; we reach out and touch a beautiful fabric. We can say that each of these is beautiful and an occasion of encountering Beauty, and we can ask ourselves, 'Do these experiences of various kinds of Beauty have anything in common apart from touch? What is that something in each case, that comes to us through our senses?' These are questions that are fundamental in what is about to come. And, furthermore, we can know that ownership would not add anything to the beautiful.[8]

It can be said that one responds to something in the perceived sound, in the taste, in the small or sight, something which I have not manufactured or created. Given my views on subject and object, I hold that there are conditions *beyond my consciousness* that enable responsiveness to Beauty. I respond to an external reality through my own internal reality (my consciousness through my senses, through my body). This is the important subject/object distinction for which I argued earlier. To repeat, there is an ontological separation between me and the world, together with a phenomenological connection. And the ontological enables the phenomenological for fear of a radical solipsism and anthropocentrism.

Being Somewhere: Experience, Imagination, and Language

When we have the experiences we have, we are always *somewhere*. This is very clear from Annie Dillard's and Barbara Hepworth's reports that we saw in Chapter 1. Indeed it is true of everything on the planet; the somewhere-ness of anything on Earth is an obvious given. Annie Dillard speaks of exploring the neighbourhood as a primary goal of infant perception, and how easily that is forgotten. She writes, 'Some unwonted, taught pride diverts us from our original intent, which is to explore the neighborhood, view the landscape, to discover at least *where* it is that we have been so startlingly set down, if we can't learn why' (Dillard, 1974 (2013): 14) (her italics). Together with the impetus to explore the neighbourhood, *awareness* of that somewhere is not always uppermost in our minds. The awareness and obviousness of always being somewhere is transcended by what we are doing, what we are thinking about, our backgrounds and character. To be aware of the somewhere in which we are situated, we need to attend to what is around us. And this is not always easy, especially since our minds have the tendency to focus on what we are doing, or our minds wander or we bracket our surroundings. Attention and awareness belong together, and both of these are aspects of our consciousnesses, and are produced by the activities of our brains in response to the environment in which we find ourselves. Our bodies respond without our knowing always, what I have described as the first moment of intentionality, the striving towards life. Our brains are what make us aware that we are, actually, somewhere, and an assumption that we are placed in space and time is an assumption, even if unconscious, that we make in everything that we do.

Yet when we are fully noticing and fully aware, we are captured to the exclusion of everything else. The capture that takes place is a kind of bracketing activity, and can include as I have been indicating, a transient bracketing of language as conscious commentary, that is to say, as narrative. Hence our brains do not shut down through such an experience. On the contrary, they are operating at many levels, simultaneously in both primary and secondary intentionality modes. Language and narrative are back-grounded as consciousness is absorbed by its object. That is why Annie Dillard, Barbara Hepworth, and Jill Bolte Taylor could later record what happened to them.

Note that I use the term 'backgrounded' advisedly, for I am not sure of the tropes appropriate to describing the way in which our consciousnesses and minds work. If, as I have suggested earlier, there is a deep *material* connection between brain and mind and consciousness, but that a materialist/physicalist thesis cannot account for consciousness itself, then we might suppose that there is a kind of three-or even four-dimensionality to mind and consciousness. And this makes me wonder about the mind as place, as a somewhere. We talk about storing things in our minds, or something's being at the back of our minds, of retrieving a memory, about the unconscious and subconscious, all of which suggest spaciousness, and temporality which is to say, place, time, and thus somewhere.

The language of our talk inevitably holds, for us, what we believe about ourselves and the world and what we experience in the world. We shall see this shortly when we examine Sigmund Freud's response to Michelangelo's 'Moses'. Like a basket that contains both treasured and discarded objects, our language embodies what we assume to be the case, what we have been taught as well as what we have lived and observed. Sometimes, that language is used as a vehicle for expression, sometimes a means of description, sometimes a maker of reality through uttering words of promise or betrayal. Without a functioning brain, however, there is no language, and our beliefs and ideas, remembered for us, frame our return to the dust (Lyons, 2019).

While Annie Dillard remarks that a running description of the present is necessary for her to know what is happening, a position, as we saw, that she later modifies, we might also note that a running description, a narrative is, or can become, an essential part of our identity.[9] And why not? That is the kind of loquacious creature that we are. Whether or not we must always be like this, though, is what is in question here. Personal identity, as both sameness and self[10] continue once the narrative is established. It does not have to be turned on all of the time like a light illuminating our way. That is what we learn from Annie Dillard. Who we are is not entirely catchable through an examination of, or total commitment to, running narrative. The persons we are before language and before narrative continue throughout our lives, in the very reproducing cells of our bodies. We are made and re-made as living organisms between birth and death, and, as dead bodies, we exist through the living Earth. This very thought exemplifies the role of change in our lives, as I suggested above. Language and narrative reinforce our conscious being, but are not necessary conditions *sui generis* of that being.

That said, as humans, most of us are talked into existence, and once we learn to speak, we continue to talk ourselves into existence and this becomes, for many of us, a means of keeping ourselves in existence.[11] Silence, and by this I mean the absence of words and narrative, is anathema; many of us are now on constant alert to our mobile phones and social media that fill our lives with words that confirm our existences. That said, our brains do not shut down.

Our brains, as the conscious centre of our being, can do a marvellous thing: they can imagine. We imagine what has happened, what will happen, what we would have liked to have happen and didn't and what we would like for the future. Our imaginations are time machines, but they are also centres of receptivity and creativity. Our imaginations can take us beyond what we have experienced to what we cannot experience, except imaginatively. We can imagine that we are flying, what the world would be like with peace, what we would like to do or say or would have liked to have done or said. In imagining, our brains expand our awareness of what was or is or will be possible. We can imagine what happened in the past, how we would have liked it to be or not be. We use the materials of our experience to fantasise, to fictionalise, to see differently. When we are touched by the world, our imaginations are triggered either in receptivity or re-figuring what has passed. But they are also triggered to reach beyond themselves into a tactile world that enables us to create anew, with different substance and qualities, and different outcomes. If representation is, indeed, an aspect of our mental and conscious lives, it is through imagination that it is so. The thing is, that when we imagine, *we experience*. It's the brain working us, even though we are not aware that it is so doing! Experiments have shown for instance that imaging something triggers the same areas of the brain as if the subject were actually *doing* what they imagine.

If to imagine is to form an image, and if an image is a likeness, as the dictionary suggests, then the imagination is employed in making likenesses. But of what are these likenesses, likenesses? For to imagine is often to exceed the boundaries of likeness of something sensed and experienced (seen, tasted, heard, smelt, touched), to extend into the unknown, the not before previously experienced.

Consider a work of fiction like H.G. Wells' *War of the Worlds*. In order to make his narrator believable in a world invaded by alien life forms, Wells needed to experience as he wrote, he needed to *see*, to *feel*, to *touch* differently, as he put description into the mind and words of the protagonist. The narrator is astounded by what he experiences. He is touched by sights and sounds not before heard. His perception of morality needed to change as did his perception of safety, community, and the possibility of physical transformation. The apparent barbarism of the Martians in capturing humans whom they use as a source of food might be based upon human carnivore practices, but the very idea that humans would be gathered, harvested as it were, is revolting to the narrator. So Wells took what had been experienced, and imagined something other and something other than what was morally and socially acceptable: in some ways what Wells wrote was very like the human condition, but because he invented Martians who did what we humans do, he disguised the truth of human behaviour and habits. Likeness and imagination marry each other.

The transcendent is not anything other than consciousness. Our brains are parts of our bodies. From our brains come our ideas, thoughts, imaginings, sensings. If our brains fail, we begin to cease existing to ourselves. To others, we might be a physical presence, a head, trunk, limbs that perhaps work or perhaps not. We might sit, or lie, for weeks, months, years barely moving, or, possibly, motionless, bathed in our urine and faeces, bathed in the uncomprehending stares of strangers who look into our blank faces that struggle to express an inner turmoil or acceptance. Those very bodies we all might become, in illness, towards dying and death, have experienced Beauty and Art and Nature. We maybe talked about these aspects of the world, of *our* worlds, uplifted by each day and night with their changes, with their suns and moons and grey skies and blue, with huge, puffy clouds, with their spring flowers and summer vegetables.

Imagination is responsible for the development of computers. Men have modelled computers on selected human mental activities, thinking in particular. Computers are programmed to move from point to point, logically, based on ones and zeros. And this is the source of the dualism that begins to permeate our lives.

What we do need to identify is our place in the world and both our separateness and our immersion. We sense, we feel, because of the world—natural or not—not in spite of the world. Hence touch enacts the mutual engagement of the subject and the world in two ways: inter-subjectively and through the non-subjective other. We might be selves in the complexity that is a web of human to human relations, but that web of relations exists always in the wide domain of an animating world: the natural and built environments which embed us in the web of existence in and beyond us. We are present to flora and fauna, to buildings, rocks, mountains, rivers and oceans, ice and snow, sand and sun, and to the stars. We can come to know only small parts of this immense whole. Artists, when they make their Art, capture some aspect, no matter how literal or how abstract, of this immensity. In other words, they have some aspect of the other, what is not their subjectivity.

The capture always and everywhere refers to, and derives meaning from whom, where and what we are in the situation of our being as maker or as audience. Our situation moves and changes. Our consciousnesses are moved and changed by our metamorphosing situations. Once we see that change is implicit in our subjectivities, time becomes a relevant category. Movement and time take us as touched and touching subjects through beginnings, middles, and ends. In their case, artists think about their Art projects, do/make them, reflect on their doing/making, reflect on their results. They make changes; they throw out or away what they do not want. We, the audiences, do not know of much of this: we see an end product, a performance, a picture on a wall, a building, a poem, but we, too are affected by time and the changes it brings with it. This can be seen especially in the case of fashion and trends. What was interesting and beautiful once can become old fashioned and boring. The lives of artists affect us all. We are, each one of us, so formed by our own histories that our ways of being in the world are constantly challenged and reinforced as well, but not always transformed. The touch of the artists is the touch of creativity par excellence. The artist, the maker of the beautiful, the ugly, the conceptual and symbolic, is the cultural expressor of/for us.

There is an interesting contrast here that directly encompasses the idea of change as a central factor in human consciousness.

Language and intentionality are intertwined. So let me take up the theme of the non-narrative in the context of deliberation and intentionality. Firstly, I want to point out that 'non-narrative' does not mean complete silence, but rather, absence of internal dialogue or story-telling. Hence one might be listening to a piece of music or bird song, or a roaring wind, completely immersed in the sensory wonder of sound, without an accompanying series of words from our narrative registers of which we are so fond. Our consciousnesses are deeply engaged or directed towards the object to which one is listening. However, that does not always mean that there is deliberate intent to so listen, although undoubtedly if Felix Mendelssohn's 'Italian Symphony' comes on the radio, you might stop and attend.

Yet consider this scenario: you are walking in the bush and come across the magnificent song of a magpie. You might say to yourself, 'Ah, the magpie: glorious! beautiful!' but then you might become so involved in the purity and Beauty of the sound that words cease. Narration stops. One might say immersion starts at the moment narration stops. Subject (oneself) and object (the sound of birdsong) become one. So what that does mean is that there are no accompanying words, no story being told 'inside the head' so to speak. Silence is an internal matter, something happening inside one's consciousness, rather than being a fact of the matter in the world. Sensory awareness fills one with no room for words or a story to be told. The narrative, simple words, which was an intrusion for Annie Dillard, interrupted her state of immersion. It was not an external narrative, but one that rose from her disposition to relate, as she tells us. But then she comes up with a narrative to tell us about what has happened, as I have already pointed out, post factum.[12]

Notes

1 I use the terms 'the beautiful' and 'Beauty' interchangeably depending on context.
2 For a very good summary of 'Beauty' see Sartwell (2017).
3 See Christopher Janaway's interesting discussion of Plato in Gaut and Lopes (2013), Chapter 1.
4 Socrates is Plato's voice in these dialogues, at least, that is what I take to be the case.
5 I am sticking here to the uncapitalised 'beauty' as it appears in the translation.
6 For an excellent discussion of *Pheadrus* see Reeve (Summer 2016 Edition).
7 Try this: think of a special moment when you had an unusual and uplifting insight. Then tell a friend or acquaintance, tell a few friends or acquaintances, and see how they react. My bet is that they will know exactly what you're talking about. Relating a response to a piece of music you loved in your youth, heard years later, often works in this regard.

8 Imagine that you owned the Mona Lisa. Would your ownership make it more beautiful? If so, how and why, you might ask. It is hard to countenance the idea that something is beautiful because of ownership, *because it is mine*.

9 For opposing views on this see Ricoeur (1991, 2012) and Strawson (2004).

10 This distinction is from Paul Ricoeur. See Ricoeur (1991)

11 I acknowledge that some people are deaf or hearing impaired from birth and do not develop identity through narrative as I am suggesting here. That does not mean that the deaf or hearing impaired are devoid of identity. See McDonald (2014), Mugeere et al., 2015, Najarian (2008), and Ohna (2004). This is one of the areas in which touch becomes central.

12 As a small experiment, the reader might like to concentrate say on her breathing, or noises around her, and might note that if narration or word production ceases, then she is fully immersed, and that if she begins to think, then immersion cease.

4

ART AND ITS FUNCTIONS

Some Comments About Freud and Jung

I have been arguing that the other, as either inter-subjective or non-animate world, pre-exists the self, and the sense of self we have as subjects. It is the kind of interaction between the individual self and world considered as a whole that brings a special dimension to our experience as subjects. We remain always in the world, all of us. But, and in my view, there are moments, partly constituted by difference, partly constituted by change and time, that shift from our full enclosure in the now as it were to another level. These are moments of transcendence. We shift our gaze, we step back, we take up a position with respect to the object that comes under our gaze or even into our auditory range. Recall that Dan Zahavi distinguishes between what the object is like for the subject and what the experience of the object is like. As I see it, we know what the experience is like in the movement of transcendence.

How does this work? Let's imagine that you are an artist, painting a picture or making a sculpture. You are totally engrossed in what you are doing, moving around, checking sketches, diagrams, looking for appropriate colours, materials, surfaces. Your mind and your body are one. You are looking, thinking, observing, feeling. What your Art work, the object, is like for you at this stage involves the thing under construction and your whole sentient body. A moment comes, when you break away from your immersion in the object: you stand back and look at what you are doing: you experience the object with distance and a different eye, perhaps with a critical mindset. This is a moment of transcendence, meaning that you cross over to another perspective that brings with it an alternative view and invests the Art object with its own integrity. Or is it?

Overall, however, such moments tell us what we are like, individually, and what the world is like apart from ourselves; what we humans have done that is splendid or terrible; and sometimes, both splendid and terrible. 2019 saw the fiftieth anniversary and celebration of the first steps of a human being onto the moon: this was an existential moment for the humans as a whole. We can ask ourselves: What

DOI: 10.4324/9780429022975-5

moral impact did that have, and was there a moral impact at all? What changed for us? Was human flourishing enhanced by this event? Or is the opposite the case? As I remarked earlier, we are animals in Nature who have learned to transform and to make and remake the world around us in practical and in pleasing, symbolic, ways. We bring ourselves, as makers, to using the earth and its riches. Art involves the transformative and symbolic action of humans; there is a what that is transformed as object of transformation; and there is a who, a subject, transformed in the very process of object transformation. The 'who' can be either or both maker and audience. Without that 'what', the stuff, there is no transformation.

Fundamentally, Art is about symbolic transformation. We develop ways in which we invest the handling of materials—sound, words, paint, clay—with meaning that is beyond the materials themselves, and which involves our consciousnesses in specific ways. Those ways, often systematised and socially recognisable, are creative representations of something that cannot be expressed in the materials themselves. In other words, symbolic transformation is to be understood as meta-activity. Although we have a range of views on what Art is: something grand, something found in galleries and museums and churches and public buildings and theatres and books and in public works; something small and complex and intricate and delicate like jewellery or miniatures, the symbolic is implicated in all of these ways of understanding. From the socially symbolic (the decision to place an object in an Art museum) to the religiously symbolic (a biblical depiction in a painting), 'Art' has a number of different ways of being understood. Historically, 'Art' is a concept that has arisen to describe human activity of a certain kind. It is a retrospective concept insofar as we invest the term with the creative riches of the past.

However, it is not unfair to say that what we think Art is, either deliberately constructed to be Art, or otherwise, is Art. We might hold that the making of Art involves intention and a certain understanding of what one is doing. Yes, I agree: Art is intentional transformation, but in the late eighteenth and into this century, 'Art' itself has been transformed with the heightened awareness of subjectivity. What we take now to be 'Art' was once not considered to be so. Indeed the term is recent in invention and application, filled as it has been by what we now understand poets and painters and writers and sculptors and architects to have been doing all along (Eco, 2002; Berger, 1972).

Poetry, galleries, churches, museums and their contents, theatre and books, photographs and sculpture, each of them is the product of human ingenuity, skill, and imagination. They are evidence of the transformative power we humans have. They share attributes of the experience I described. So on this understanding, it may well be the case that what I have described above could be captured by the term 'Art'.

I have noted that humans intentionally create. But we are not the only creatures that create as many of us realise, for so do bees and ants and birds and the great apes. Animals create when they make and use tools, when they build, when they burrow. But humans seem to be the only group which creates beyond the evolutionary drives all animals possess. We humans collect and forage and protect; but we also clothe ourselves, adorn our bodies, leave images that reflect the natural world, and develop symbolic systems that record and speak to our sense of the ephemeral and the unknown. Creativity, and imagination that accompanies it, are part of the bed-rock of being human. And both Art and narrative play a role here.

How important is narrative to Art? Narrative is either intrinsic to Art (poetry, literature) or an accompaniment (analysis, discussion, explanation, invitation). Can one attend to an work of Art without attempting to evoke or develop, significance or meaning through narrative? Is there either experience or language that can attend to an Art work as an work of Art, lets an work of Art speak for itself, and not be caught up in the semantic folds that embed and are simultaneously, beyond, the work of Art? Indeed, is there an work of Art behind and beyond semantic folds? My provisional answer to these questions is 'yes'. Ontologically, the beyond-ness of the artwork in itself is inescapable, even in this age when we seem to think that everything is reducible to human perception, individual opinion, and consciousnesses. So it is with these questions that I begin my exploration of Art in the context of Nature and Beauty.

Another question: Have you ever noticed that many people who visit Art Galleries have a tendency to glance at a work of Art and spend more time reading the artist's statement, or a description/interpretation of the work of Art? As a colleague has pointed out, this is the case with abstract Art in particular, where meaning and significance are not immediately obvious. Historically, works of Art: paintings, sculptures, music, told stories were narrative in intent. Many people were illiterate and visual Art acted as an *aide-memoire* (e.g. moral behaviour and lessons to be learned) and as an inspiration. Indeed, stories were both depicted and reiterated through different forms of Art: visual art and music in particular which reinforced what was preached from the pulpit.

So Art has a function, and its function has varied across cultures and through time. Modern scripts such as artist statements help to realise that function. The makers of Art might intentionally seek to shock, to alter perceptions, to make people think, as might those who employ artists, the patrons and commissioners of Art pieces. Art might also function to embody memory of great persons and/or to display their wealth and power. In Western history, the Church has been particularly influential in this regard.

The pulpit, religious themes, myths and ancient, heroic stories have often been deployed as ciphers, as symbols and meaning makers through Art. These now have a diminished presence or even absence, in modern secular societies. For example, many of us do not know the stories of the Bible, and the threat of the Last Judgement and hell; we do not know about the exploits of Odysseus or Boadicea. We do not think much about angels or devils unless it is through popular fantasy/fiction, although, undoubtedly, that medium is influenced by old stories and Art history. Regardless, the horror on the faces of the damned in, for example, Michelangelo's *Last Judgement* in the Sistine Chapel, was meant to be something to be looked at, to learn by and from. Imagery told a story, and imagery without words talked to the soul of the spectator; but words might have provided a back-drop to the eidetic experience. Seeing and looking functioned to teach and also to enhance, and also to deter. Yet words, narrative, had already functioned to inform the spectator about what was being depicted.

In the case of the Church, preaching enabled listeners not only to be instructed but also provided the narrative story-telling so important to triggering the imagination of the listener. There is a sense, then, in which gallery visitors are engaging in secular and aesthetic instruction similar to their forebears' experience, when they read artists' statements. However, the representational element of Art and here I mean representation of the Natural world and mimicry of human figures, is absent in many modern works. The development of abstract Art, especially visual Art, and the turn away from representation and narrative to (self-) expression highlights this difference. Abstract Expressionism, for example, treated the unconscious as a source for the activity of painting, a spontaneous invocation of the power of paint splashed onto a canvas, perhaps willy-nilly. Jackson Pollock's abstract work, 'Blue Poles' (www.nma.gov.au/defining-moments/resources/blue-poles), is in stark contrast to works such as 'The Sons of Clovis' (Luminais, Art Gallery of NSW Australia) or 'The Last Judgement' (Michaelangelo, Sistine Chapel, Rome, Italy) or 'The Raft of the Medusa' (Géricault, Louvre, Paris, France).

That said, one might need a narrative to 'get' not only Abstract Expressionist works, but many Art works, abstract or not. However, what one 'gets' may not be a story with a theme. Rather, one can be introduced to, and perhaps confounded by paint on a canvas, by the play of light and water in a James Turrell installation, by an elongated figure in a Giacometti sculpture, by the discordant, repetitive sounds of the music of composer Steve Reich. Artists' statements, and sometimes their writings, explain or clarify or illuminate, their Art. So their narratives are about intent, about method and about their psyches, often in the context of social critique. Nor is narrative omitted in deliberately political Art such as Social Realism. There is a political, consciousness-raising point to be made, an aim to indoctrinate. Thus narrative is not completely omitted. Artists' statements, and here I might add the vested interests of political masters, are, rather, a *shift* in narrative. In some cases, the shift is primarily from the subject matter of the painting to the subjectivity of the painter, to the painter's method, aims, philosophy, and politics. In some cases, however, it is a way of insisting on a political position, of reinforcing deeply held beliefs and commitments, a secular, political, reiteration of religious practice from hundreds of years ago into the present.

The point I am making is that observers need to be able to understand, to find meaning and significance in what is before their eyes, or engaging their listening. Without a narrative in the form of, for example, an artist's statement, understanding is limited. The statement thus provides a way of seeing anew precisely because many of us do not *see*, or *understand*; we cannot look or listen, do not or cannot apprehend, or do not know how to. This seems like a strange situation, does it not, when we cannot apprehend, or do not know how to? As far as I can see, then, narrative and Art were, and continue to be, companions. So the question is then raised about the very possibility of engaging in Art without narrative as either its companion or in its story-telling context.

Recall that I suggested, earlier, that 'Art' is to be understood as the expression and articulation of relationships that we have to both the Natural and engineered or built environments in which we live. Hence the term 'Art' connotes visual, auditory and literal representations and imaginative re-figuring of the contexts in which we find ourselves. Recall also, that I claimed that 'Beauty' is to be understood as the existence in an object (something other than a perceiving subject), or of an arrangement of parts, such that a special kind of happy feeling is evoked that has to do directly with the object. That happy feeling, I claimed, is positively transformational and uplifting. The encounter between subject and object is such that one feels better.

From what I have been arguing here, however, it appears that we need to remind ourselves that Art is not always beautiful: skilful, painted, or sculpted, well or even badly, discordant, overly loud music, clumsy, frenetic dancing are hardly occasions of Beauty, yet they are considered to be Art. Art and Beauty can complement each other, but Beauty is not what makes Art, Art. Art is made by humans in an endeavour to show something about the world or, in this age of self-expression, themselves. Art is a human endeavour, a way of symbolic presentation that uses a range of materials and activities (paint, clay, instruments, sound, writing, movement) and intentions, all of which involve touch. As I have just indicated, Art has many functions.

But as we found with Beauty, Art, too, is also exceptionally difficult to define or fully characterise. Additionally, I am not sure if coming up with a definition of something adds anything to our *experience* of that something. If we intuitively respond to something and can say that we are responding because it's beautiful or an exquisite work of Art (or repulsive although a work of Art) then that might be enough. The experience of having our senses engaged has aroused us already, and definition seems extraneous. And having our senses aroused implies change, alteration of perception and experience.

Where narrative is in play, our responses to Art are mediated by some dimension of narrative for both artist and observer, albeit differently. The concerns of each do not need to match: the artist intends while the observer comprehends, say, with an emphasis on colour on the one hand, and overall impression on the other. That seems clear from what I have been arguing. And narrative permeates our lives from the very beginning, as I have already remarked. My question, then, about the possibility of engaging in Art without narrative is salient.

In my view, suspension implies temporary absence rather than total erasure. After all, Annie Dillard *later* wrote about what had happened to her. Our capacity to narrate seems to operate in the background even when it is not actively telling us something or being called on to tell something to someone else. The making/using/recalling (of) narrative indicates that this capacity is not linear or one-dimensional. Just as language function operates across the brain (https://theconversation.com/what-brain-regions-control-our-language-and-how-do-we-know-this-63318) so narrative permeates both our conscious and unconscious. Even if we do not have scripts 'written' into our brains, our memories are such that we create narratives to talk about the past and envision the future. That is what is important here, for all of us.

Yet spontaneity *qua* spontaneity need not have a supporting narrative. One catches a glimpse of a beautiful combination of sound or colour, or one squeezes paint from the tube in just the right place, or brings together the 'right' notes as if driven by a creative insight. What makes this rightness might not be discoverable, even with empirical investigation which could involve controlled studies that cannot capture the spontaneity of a moment. Yet it is also possible to develop a narrative that explains or elucidates a work of Art apart from spontaneity or that underpins a work of Art right from the start: that is how religious themes operate. Origins are interesting. Some of us demand to know where something came from or how an artist made the work that they made.

So to return to my opening question: can a work of Art speak for itself, merely because it is a work of Art? If narrative is as important as I have been indicating, then how do we answer this question except by denying that it can? For we might wonder how do a display of colour with or without form, shape, figure, or a lump of clay, or a piece of marble, or words on a page, or sounds, or creativity and imagination get to be works of Art in the first place? Is it because that something is in a church, or an Art Gallery or on public display in a city square, say? Does *place*, where something is, render that something Art? If we think of any Art work, we might be inclined to say, 'Yes' place is of special importance. Along with this view agreement amongst artists, critics, commentators subtends the designation 'Art', because, clearly, sociocultural context is important: fashion, expectation, novelty, conservatism, sensibility. And what if there is no consensus? The *Salon des Refusés* in Paris in 1863 is a case in point. Then again, does something have to be *liked* in order to be Art? Hardly, for one can say that a piece is skilful, well executed, designed well, balanced, and yet not like that something even though it is considered Art. An Art work can be rejected by an individual or by a community, for example, because it does not fit with the current sensibility or *morés* around the particular Art concerned (as was the case with the *Paris Salon* (*Académie royale de peinture et de sculpture*) for which tradition was extremely important. For the residents of Fitzroy, Victoria, Australia, Adam Stone's 'Fallen Fruit', a skull-topped half-peeled steel and fibre-glass banana, is such a case. Skill can be appreciated in the absence of liking. The attributes of works of Art very often include just those properties (and maybe even more) I listed above. This seems to suggest that human feeling is not the sole criterion for judging a work to be 'Art'. Art can be Art regardless of liking or disliking and regardless of skill.

Of course both liking and disliking something are directly connected with our emotions and we may like something because we do actually judge it to be pleasing rather than having a gut reaction. A key word here is the idea of judgement: we judge something to be or not to be, Art. If this is the case, the use of the term 'Art' is largely conventional. The point though, is that we respond to something as Art, always within a context, framed by expectations, experience, and knowledge. Carl Jung argues for a strong complementarity between religion and Art, between history, war and Art; the context, what embeds Art (and what Art embeds), is crucial. He recognises the importance of the relationship between what Nietzsche calls the Dionysian and Apollinian and says, 'A true understanding is possible only on common ground—no one would wish to maintain that the nature of a railway bridge is adequately understood from a purely aesthetic angle' (Jung, 1990: 141).

A work of Art speaks for itself through the emotional connection it makes to an observer, and the response elicited. The narrative puzzles we observers might have, predispose against, or even disallow, this speaking for itself, yet, at the same time, the narrative puzzles contribute to the emotional connection. As we shall see, Sigmund Freud understood this. Basically, we *can* disconnect ourselves from our senses by focusing on what our reason demands which in this case might, in effect, be a proscription of emotional response.

Through our senses, Art touches our emotional psyches, as do Nature and Beauty: our brains, and sometimes, our whole bodies, respond. Through our rational psyches, we can mediate those responses, make sense, give significance, give meaning. Emotion and reason can work together; or they might not. That is part of the point of the distinction between the Dionysian and the Apollinian. Whatever is the case, senses are primary: they come first, since touch, in the way in which I have outlined it, is an original mediator of our psychic lives. One wonders, however, if the experience of Art is as full as it can be if one does disengage emotionally, if the focus of enjoyment is on narrative rather than the Art itself? If one *reads* rather than experiences (takes in, becomes emotionally involved), for example, the Beauty of colour or the story behind the opera or piece of music, what is it that one is actually experiencing? As far as rational response to Art is concerned, in which narrative frames appreciation and understanding, there are some remarkable cases from the point of view of the observer. Sigmund Freud is a case in point so it is with him that I start.

Michaelangelo's 'Moses'

Here is Sigmund Freud. He is visiting *San Pietro in Vincoli*, a colonnaded Basilica in Rome. Inside, he is gazing at Michaelangelo's 'Moses', which is, for him, a puzzle. We get the idea that Freud remains before Moses for a long time, lost in contemplation. Now Freud is writing and he tells us that although he is a layman when it comes to Art, '(n)evertheless works of art do exercise a powerful effect on me, especially those of literature and sculpture, less often painting'. Freud says that he tries to work out the effect such works have on him and he spends time *apprehending* them. When he cannot do that, he is 'almost incapable of obtaining pleasure'. Why is that the case? Because, he says, '(s)ome rationalistic, or perhaps analytic, turn of mind in me rebels against being moved by a thing without knowing why I am thus affected and what it is that affects me' (Freud, 1914: 211). Freud's intellect, his rational psyche is the mediator of his appreciation of 'Moses'. His is, primarily, an intellectual apprehension and he does not seem to consider how his senses inform his apprehension. For him, it is not the Art *per se* that is the puzzle. It is its meaning, or so we might think. His apprehending a work of Art is an intellectual problem, something that goes on in his head, a problem to be solved rationally: 'apprehension' is after all, an aspect of intellectual cognition. He cannot let the work speak for itself, bring itself to him as a sensual experience without the intervention of reason. But for him, the intellect is an aid to his interpreting a work of Art.

Freud's will to narrate is strong because he needs to understand and to interpret the sculpture, and its effect on him. In attempting to find a meaning, he moves from the thing before him to his own mind in *which it is represented*. For Freud's search for meaning, for why he is moved by this sculpture, is irretrievably caught up in narration, in thoughts. He engages in mind talk, in analysis, in moving away from the cause of his questions if you like, to seek an answer to the questions within himself. His is an assessment of the *meaning* of the sculpture of Moses, what Moses might or might not be doing, or about to do. He appeals to other experts to get an idea of what might be the case. He does not look at the huge block of marble sculptured: hammered, chipped, soothed by the hand of Michaelangelo. He does not look at what Vasari might say, or what Ascavi Condini might add. Michael Holroyd comments of 'Moses':

> It is yet true that, although it is botched and patched up, it is the most worthy monument to be found in Rome, or, perhaps, anywhere else; if for nothing else, at least, for the three statues that are by the hand of the master: among them that most marvellous Moses, leader and captain of the Hebrews, who is seated in an attitude of thought and wisdom, holding under his right arm the tables of the law, and supporting his chin with his left hand, like one tired and full of cares. Between the fingers of that hand escape long waves of his beard—a very beautiful thing to see. And his face is full of life and thought, and capable of inspiring love and terror, which, perhaps, was the truth. It has, according to the usual descriptions, the two horns on his head a little way from the top of the forehead. He is robed and shod in the manner of the antique, with his arms bare. A work most marvellous and full of art, and much more so because all the form is apparent beneath the beautiful garments with which it is covered. The dress does not hide the shape and beauty of the body, as, in a word, may be seen in all Michael Angelo's clothed figures, whether in painting or sculpture. The statue is more than twice the size of life.
>
> *Holroyd, 1903*

Freud appears to endorse Holroyd's opinion, and his own experience of 'Moses' is mediated by his intellect, and by the intellects of the critics to whom he does appeal. Freud is more interested in the story, more interested in what is going on, in the context of the statue, its association with the Exodus story, its interpretation of that story. He is not interested in the piece of marble, in the smoothness of lines, in the drapery, in the talent and craftsmanship that made 'Moses'.

We have, here, a kind of confessional account of an omnipotence of thinking and thoughts which, obviously, narrative involves. The power of narrative should not be underestimated; nor should its absence in some cases, though. And Freud spends much of his essay recounting the thoughts of others about 'Moses' and objecting to what they say. It seems to me that he is trying to get at the 'truth' of the 'inscrutable' statue and is profoundly dissatisfied with commentary and analysis offered by critics.

For Freud, without intellectual apprehension there is no pleasure. The intellect, as a mediator, plays a causal role in his being moved, and he *is* moved by the statue. From what he says, he is resistant to immediacy, resistant to tumbling into emotion, to untrammelled feeling and this reveals the importance of narrative to his appreciation. Freud needs his intellect as a mediator of pleasure. He *needs* thought. Freud is telling us that he *will not*, rather than cannot feel without explanation of what it is that he is feeling. Indeed he inhibits feeling: his mind rebels and his resistance brings to the fore the imperative to narrate, to decide through judgement, what is the case, the real story behind the posture of Moses. Pleasure comes to him through understanding and reason, through knowing. His sensuous, responding body is bracketed as he concentrates on what is going on what can be said about the statue, the story behind Moses' posture. Light into his eyes, the surroundings, the setting of the sculpture, the smell and temperature of the church are bracketed as if they might not contribute to Freud's pleasure. If they do, he deliberately blocks them.

It seems to me that Freud's language indicates a kind of mental ardour that is almost cantankerous: a turn of his mind rebels. He is unsure of what it is that causes the rebellion: perhaps it is a rationality or analyticity in the face of unknowing, or of ignorance. He wants to know why and what moves him in the sculpture, so yes, he is moved, but moved as an effect of figuring something out, of telling a story to himself, of narrating. He invokes the idea of authorial intention and evokes the emotional excitement of the artist:

> In my opinion, what grips us so powerfully can only be the artist's *intention* in so far as he has succeeded in expressing it in his work and in getting us to understand it. I realise that this cannot be merely a matter of *intellectual* comprehension; what he aims at is to awaken in us the same emotional attitude, the same mental constellation as that which in him produced the impetus to create.
>
> *Freud, 2001: 212, italics in original*

It is interesting that he disavows the idea that understanding the author's intention is not merely an *intellectual* matter. He wants to interpret in order to know why he is so profoundly affected. However, such an invocation is, for him, inadequate when he is trying to understand what this piece of Art is about, its meaning, in order to understand the piece of Art itself. Freud, then, does see that there is a connection between his feelings and his intellect: intellect helps to uncover the why of feeling.

That is the context of his discussion about what Art critics have said about 'Moses'. He wonders, with the critics, what moment is represented here, how it is related to the golden calf incident, whether or not Moses is about to break the tablets containing the commandments.[1] But, I wonder, is he contemplating 'Moses', the work of Art before him or what the work represents, what *it* is telling him, and us? Does 'Moses' disappear and become a means to telling a story rather than a work of Art in itself? Can 'Moses' be appreciated without that story? Or is its significance wholly tied up as a sculpture for the tomb of Julius II? Does Freud's intellect take over as he ruminates and explores the meaning of the sculpture?

Given what Freud assumes about the motive forces of artists and their potential congruency with those of an audience, we might wonder how Freud sees himself in relation to the statue as a piece of sculptured marble. After all, he writes that he has entered the church and has 'assayed to support the angry scorn of the hero's glance'.

> Sometimes I have crept cautiously out of the half-gloom of the interior as though I myself belonged to the mob upon whom his eye is turned – the mob which can hold fast no conviction, which has neither faith not patience, and which rejoices when it has regained its illusory idols.
>
> *Freud, 2001: 213*

Evidently, that this is a statue, a marvellous piece of sculptured marble, is of tremendous importance to him. This is what he confesses when he apparently engages with Moses' stern eye. Yet he is very tied up in an *accurate* interpretation of its meaning (thus his discussion of critics and other interpreters). The general point I am making here, though, is that Freud's appreciation is mediated by a narrative of which he is in control. And in that sense, he is, of course, like those of us who look at Art by taking cognisance of 'or looking at' a narrative first. So Freud is following in the tradition of his European predecessors: seeing Art through narrative seems to be our default position.

And perhaps this is what motivates all of us, as we engage in reading, in the story of an Art piece. As an example, go to *The Louvre*, and look at the multitudes of spectators clamouring in front of *Mona Lisa*. Ask yourself: Why are they there? Is it because they were walking past and suddenly came across this small but enticing portrait? Or have they gone deliberately to see what they have been *told* is the work of genius? We are told, after all, that this is the work of genius! Am I, or is anyone, primarily concerned with the play of light, the texture of paint, the colour, the balance? Or is the mystery smile and the self-possession of the subject what allures? The point is that many of us *know* something about *Mona Lisa* before we arrive, and that is what frames our responses. We interpret *because* we know. Most, maybe all of us, are unlike Annie Dillard in her pre-narrative moment of rapture before language interrupts. However, that seems like a harsh judgement when Annie Dillard herself realises that what happened to her was momentary and quite out of the blue. The unpredictability of the moment, its spontaneity interrupts the usual, the ordinary, the way in which she, and most of us, approach the world. While narrative might frame our appreciation of Art (and Nature and Beauty) it is those moments devoid of narrative that bring us enormous, unintended and surprising, insight.

Hence Freud's is one way to appreciate and to talk about Art. As an intellectual exercise, the object—the sculpture in Freud's case—relies on a mental representation, that is to say, *his* narrative about 'Moses', is informed by the mental representations of scholars and historians. They represent to Freud what they consider to be the most important aspects of the sculpture—the story of Moses and the tablets. Their representations influence Freud's understanding of what is depicted and also frame his emotional response. Representation does count, sometimes. But representation is not immediacy, it is *re-presentation*: the object comes to us, the statue comes to Freud not in itself, but as an image he has made. We always, it would seem, must slip our intellects into the picture, always mediating. Perhaps it is not fashionable to talk about the marble, the texture, the skill, the technique the artisan quality of the work. Perhaps it is more fashionable to talk about meaning and context and the life of the maker, talk that is, about narrative and representation. If so, what is being presented and what is being represented? On the interpretation I am proposing, the original, what sits in front of the eye, outside the subject's apprehension, perception, noticing, what is there, independent of the subject, is bracketed, is, indeed, 'seen' briefly, and then it is to the mind, as it narrates, and not to the presented object that one turns. The narrative mediates to produce a representation. The object, in the case of 'Moses', the statue, the Art, in itself is replaced by mind wanderings, by rumination, speculation and separation from the immediacy of the senses, which is almost disallowed.

All of that said, it is clear that language and narrative do inform much of what we do, and are. That seems indisputable. What I am questioning is the weighty, single minded, dependence that many of us have on our urge to narrate as if without narrative we would be unable to experience or could not exist. Silence, stillness of the mind, and its impulse to narrate and thus absence of words has a place. Hence I would say that we are all very like Freud: we take for granted our places in the world as a direct effect of the senses (until something goes wrong). Our bodies take us wherever we go. Our bodies are the sensuous source of all that there is for us, yet this is something we forget. We live, unconscious of our bodies for most of the time. Pain, soreness, hunger, thirst, and sexual pleasure are on-going reminders of our bodies. And we all want to narrate, to tell stories, to use words, endlessly, thoughtlessly at times. Is there a place for contemplation, silence, full sensual engagement in our lives? Yes, there always have been narratives, interpretations, stories behind, and informing works of Art. Yet beyond the historical dictates of narrative and their instrumental roles in Art, the narrative imperative has become a personal storyteller in our galleries and Art exhibitions. A landscape has a story, a portrait has a story, an impressionist work has a story directly associated with the biography of its artist: works cannot speak for themselves. Many works are not simply titled, they need a long, sometimes biographical, sometimes technical, sometimes source-of-inspiration little pieces of tell-it-all text attached nearby in case the observer is distracted by the Art work itself. And where that is not the case, a glossy booklet will perform the same job. Freud's mental preoccupation with what the sculptured Moses is doing and his discussion of critics, his resistance to letting himself be carried away by a work of Art, acts in such a way. We do not discover Freud's response to the work of Art *qua* work of Art. We do not seem to be able to do so. He will not permit it, for narrative, interpretation, words are the only avenue to seeing an art work as such?

It would seem that we would open ourselves to great psycho-social risk if we were to entirely abandon ourselves to the so-called Dionysian impulse. As a way of being in the world, to be immersed in a wholly emotional and boundless state predisposes against sense-making. Boundaries do matter (thus the importance of the Apollinian if we stick to the opposition of the two impulses). The Apollinian/Dionysian dichotomy as a description of our psychological impulses does serve the purpose of providing a way of understanding different responsive aspects of our psyches. Whether or not this dichotomy is the whole story is another matter. As Jung realised, polarities are not always so: rather, the 'partners' can be complementary, even enhancing each other. Many of us would recognise in ourselves open-ness and resistance that periodically pops up in our psyches: that is a sign of the liveliness of our minds. Freud's comments about needing his intellect to understand, while at the same time claiming that it is not all about the intellect alone, is perhaps a nuanced version of this. What Freud does not seem to be prepared to do, though, is to momentarily abandon his psyche to his emotions without a narrative framing. All three thinkers, Nietzsche, Jung, and Freud, capture the mercurial nature of the psyche as it responds or reacts according to its living environment. For Freud, resistance is intentional. Annie Dillard was not observing a work of Art: but there was no resistance in her experience. She was carried away, as someone might be in experiencing an Art work.

In *The Red Book, Liber Novus* Carl Jung accompanies a narrative with brilliant symbolic paintings (Jung et al., 2009). Colour, image, illuminated lettering, and relationship to narrative are all in evidence. The dream-like quality of many of the paintings testify to an imaginative integration of word and image. It is difficult to conceive of how Jung's work in this *magnum opus* could be interpreted wholly as narrative or wholly as image. This is not to say that one cannot appreciate *The Red Book* as a work of Art in itself. For this is an example of the marriage of word and image, an example of seeing something in itself without knowing anything more.

Actually, I do not know where to put works such as this. Yes, it *is* Art. And yes, narrative tells us the story of the Book, just as narrative does in many pieces of literature. Art comes to us in many forms. We do not have to understand music scales or engineering to be overcome by the Art of music or architecture. The experience of Art, like the experience of Beauty and Nature, brings the whole self into focus through altered realisation of one's Being, one's possibilities.

That does not answer questions about Art as Art. That is not possible to answer without adumbrating theory after theory after theory, often by persons who are not creators, but have relationships parasitic on Artists. Artists know who they are. Or maybe they do not. Jung did not know, or admit to being an artist (Frank, 2013). But it possibly does answer the question with which I began this chapter: narrative is exceptionally important to Art. But so is silence, loss of words, being gob-smacked by Beauty and Nature. Indeed being gob-smacked, lost for words, momentarily erased even is one of the pinnacle experiences of human Being, of being Human.

And touch is what underpins all of these activities, all of these experiences. We are touched by, and touch the world. And with that, comes responsibility.

Nothing else to say here … for the moment. Human flourishing comes next.

Note

1 There are many discussions and critiques of Freud's essay on 'Moses'; see, for example, Bergstein (2006), Bremer (1976), Macmillan and Swales (2003).

5

NATURE, BEAUTY, ART

Foundations of an Ethical Life

In *Jung and Levinas: An Ethics of Mediation* I maintained that awareness of the mother, a kind of maternal pre-cognition on the part of the foetus, is the primary mode of awareness, an awareness that is sensuous and sensible rather than cognitive. This I claimed, is ultimately, the foundation of ethics. I still believe this. But I also believed, and still do, that an unrecognised, pre-cognitive, partner of ethics is the fact of our beginnings in Nature. Yet paradoxically, we come to Nature cognitively, *after* we come to the mother. An aspect of this paradox is that the mother is part of Nature, as are we. The paradox concerns the sequential awareness we develop as we grow older and learn to distinguish ourselves from o/Others. Our learning to use language, to narrate and distinguish different aspects of this multifarious world, is fundamental in this. It enables these basic forms of cognition and then recognition. That we are sensuous, sensible, individuals both separate from, and intertwined with, the human world and with Nature, is something we learn *because of* our sensuousness, because of our conscious materiality and because of language learning and use. Together, these elements form the basis of individuation. For us, narrative, itself dependent on language, is a kind of prime mover for framing the world and our experience. We find the importance of narrative across most of our human endeavours, including our psychological growth towards individuation.

Psychological therapies that include taking cognisance of the situatedness of individuals that do not lay 'blame' at the feet of individuals are a necessity for a just collective, of any kind, small or large, a segment, or the whole. To reiterate, our formation in the female body as a 'tissue of sensation' (Dillard, 1974 (2013): 203) creates a mutual sensitivity that is expressed in the mother–child relationship but which is then extended beyond that primal relationship into our growth as human beings in sociocultural worlds. Sociocultural worlds are dependent on us, as we are dependent on them. Yet we come into this world without self-conscious awareness, and it is our response to our worlds that subsequently initiates and creates ourselves

DOI: 10.4324/9780429022975-6

and our subjectivity. In other words, the o/Other—thought here of the world and Other selves in it—is instrumental in the production of subjectivity. Our pre-reflective consciousness is always engaged with and in the world, but because of the limits of our physical immaturity, we never know this as a form of first-person subjectivity. The touch, the sound, the smell, the taste of the o/Other, in all of its manifestations, is what brings us to our conscious awareness of ourselves. When we begin to think, to act, to speak, we begin to come into ourselves as self-conscious beings, capable of moral agency. We use language; we learn to narrate; and we learn to be silent. This is the becoming of us as moral agents. We are full moral agents when we cease to blame the o/Other for our failures, for what we do not understand, when we take responsibility for who and what we are, when we withdraw projections. The latter is an important lesson from Jung, and also from Buddhism (Sogyal, 1992).

Recall that Carl Jung argued that individuation is a process of differentiation. The goal, he argues, is 'the development of the individual personality'. Jung argues that the relationship between individual and collective is reciprocal to the extent that where there is a stunted collective, there are stunted individuals (Jung, 1990: 448). By implication, the freedom of individuals will have an impact on the collective. But there is a balance, perhaps fragile, there to be honoured. In my view, freedom of the individual must always be mediated by the effect the individual has on the collective; and the collective must always be aware of the effect of its decisions, rules, and practices, on the individual. Much of this is embedded in narrative. Repression and/or oppression is neither good for individual nor collective. Human flourishing—of individual and collective—must complement and, indeed, enhance each o/Other. In order for this to be the case, both individuals and collective must withdraw projections, withdraw, that is, the prejudices and biases they have towards the objectified o/Other. Arguably, racism, sexism, cultural phobias, and stereotyping all involve projection of the psychologically undesirable. But human flourishing is dependent upon the flourishing of non-human Nature, so projection around Nature needs also to be addressed.

Indeed, one of the principal projections many humans foster is that humans are independent of Nature. We project the contents of our psyches onto a natural world we do not understand and to which, as intelligent, minded humans, we feel superior. If Jung is right about projection then, what we are in effect doing is ridding ourselves of our awareness of our mortality, our dependency, inferiority, and fragility, in other words, what we do not like to admit about ourselves. We do not always do this consciously, deliberately. However, narrative plays a key role here. This is expressed in philosophical positions such as metaphysical dualism. But it is not a position confined to philosophy. We can see it in our refusal to accept, for example, the human contribution to global warming through the destruction of environment and habitat. When we repeatedly blame others for their assumed faults without any self-examination or reflection, we are also engaging in projective practice. To realise our propensity to project and then the possibility of withdrawal is a major step in individuation and is thus a moment of potential ethical insight and transformation. Suspension of our narrative mode of being in moments of insight can be productive in this process.

While narrative enacts our separateness, non-narrative moments such as that had by Annie Dillard enact our one-ness, our continuity. This is not always the case: one can be with a crowd, speechless or out of place, and feel entirely separate, lost for words as it were. The interplay between narrative and non-narrative and the moments they embody can be fluid, of course. The way in which Annie Dillard's awareness moved swiftly from immersion to seeing her immersion and reusing narrative in her later text demonstrates this. From what Dillard writes, we can say that Nature and Beauty together helped her to realise something that is directly involved in the individuation process. Their effect, either separately or together, beyond narrative moved her, changed her, gave her a moment of profound realisation. Her Art is expressed, though, in the narrative of the moment about which she later writes. In this she used reason as a developmental tool for her artistic expression. Her recognising that 'this is it', although an interruption to her experience of completeness, oneness, is a positive insertion of her rationality, a kind of narrative summing up, a narrative revelation of what was the case for her.

The heightened feeling of such moments together with the after-realisation, the insight gained, founds an existential determination which is at once personal and more broadly, a desire to act better in the world. Such a desire is the basis of ethics. As living creatures, we humans, generally speaking, strive towards being, existentially, *and towards being good*. 'Being good' is an affirmation of our human relationships and presents the possibility of loving ease in the world. The specific aspect of psychological transformation in the process of individuation, based on both feelings and experiences of wholeness, and a desire for human flourishing is what makes our lives ethical or moral lives. Echoing Jung, we can say that human flourishing cannot happen without wholeness, without a sense that each human individual has responsibility not only to herself, but to her community, and even towards those she does not love. Wholeness is a feature of Nature, of the fabric of being. It is something towards which someone strives when they are miserable, bereft, broken, or lost. The striving is a psychological and transformative search for happiness or human flourishing (Greek: *eudaimonia*)[1] which we might think of as an existential pilgrimage.

Jung's contention that where there is a stunted collective, there are stunted individuals, has repercussions not only for psychic health, but for moral health. His definition of *collective* attests to this:

> I term *collective* all psychic contents that belong not to one individual but to many, i.e., to a society a people, or to mankind *(sic)* in general. Such contents are what Lévy-Bruhl calls the *representations collectives* of primitives, as well as general concepts of justice, the state, religion, science, etc., current among civilized man *(sic)*.
>
> *Jung, 1971: 417*

Note that Jung includes justice, not only a political but most certainly, a moral concept within this definition. I cited Jung's claim that there is a reciprocal relation between collective and individuals, viz. that where there are stunted individuals, there will be a stunted collective. The experience of individuals is not always a direct result of our being in the collective as epiphanic experience suggests. Reason and our ability to transcend, to take a 'view from above'[2] through conscientious, committed practice results in the ability to see differently. Jung himself acknowledges that transcendence, as what he calls 'function', is a complex of psychic functions. We can utilise our psychic functions, or they can utilise us depending on what is going on, to achieve ends outside what might be expected to conform to collective thinking. That is how collective change happens. The insight of individuals can have a direct transformative effect on the collective (witness both Freud and Jung in this regard: but the whole of human history is dotted with examples....). In other words, we can use the complexity of the psyche to transform both ourselves and our collectives, our groups and communities.[3]

Without invoking a body/soul ontological distinction, we might learn from the Greeks and their idea of the view from above. Metaphorically speaking, the soul can grow wings and fly, see what cannot be seen from where we currently are, take a 'view from above'. Compare this with the contrast between being in a valley and looking down on that same valley from a mountain or cliff-top. The connection between transcendence and view from above is plain: we need to direct our minds, our thinking, away from mundane concerns in which we are involved, and attempt to see differently. We do this by contemplating our mortality, recognising what is important and what trivial. Figuring out necessary and trivial aspects of our lives is an age-old philosophical search, from the Greek Stoics, Epicureans, and Sceptics to Buddhist philosophies. What are the most desirable and productive human goals remains as a great problem, personal, political, and moral, today in this contemporary world (Nussbaum, 2011, 2013; Smith, 1904). But we can also do this in epiphanic moments, those times existential insight devoid of narrative but full of sensual engagement.

Jung's inclusion of justice as a content of collectives is interesting considering that very few collectives manifest justice. Suppose that justice is a necessary condition of a flourishing sociocultural group, then that collective would not be stunted. But the opposite is the case: most collectives are stunted both from a broad and narrow or personal perspective. Even cultures that have champions who propose how to live a good life can be lacking in justice. Consider, for example, Marcus Aurelius' *Meditations.* They are a wonderful read: they are inspiring. They give us a view of what is possible as a human being: don't waste your energies on either the past or the future over which you have no control. Consider only what is within your moral domain, the only thing over which you have any control. One might wonder to whom these exhortations might apply considering the fact that Marcus Aurelius was a Roman Emperor, the ruler of an Empire founded on murdering, raping, and enslaving whole groups of people across Europe, East, and West. Slaves were also thought of human beings, worthy of respect. Yet we might wonder, material conditions brought to the forefront, whether they truly apply to slaves, to women, to those who are conquered when 'dignity is the only thing of true importance to human flourishing' (Nussbaum, 2013: 505). It seems to me that telling a slave, pregnant to her master, to forget about the past, there is nothing to be done, to not imagine a future for it is beyond your control, and to focus on being indifferent to indifferent things (viz. that over which you have no control) is cant. Where is justice and the recognition that our material circumstances have a direct impact on our happiness, here?

I am assuming that without justice, a collective/group/society is stunted, and that Jung was also supposing the importance of justice. If that is the case, then the absence of justice reflects on the whole collective, not merely local groups, but universally. However, the actual acknowledgement that all humans *are* human beings, and deserve to be treated in the best possible way in order to promote flourishing can appear to be merely aspirational, and aspirational for only some at that.[4] Where imperialist expansionism, hatred, racism, sexism, religious discrimination, and all forms of oppression and lack of recognition occur, it is clearly the case that human flourishing of the totality of the collective is not at the forefront of either moral or political practice (and belief). Our recognition of our place in Nature, that we are in Nature, the play of Beauty in our lives and how it makes us feel and behave admirably, and how Art promotes these are all fundamental to flourishing because they do not stunt, either personally or collectively.

Nature, Art, Beauty help us to realise our limitations as well as our expansive possibilities. So that while feeling one-ness with the cosmos, narrative abandoned, brings with it a feeling of wholeness, the mundanity of most of our lives is always framed by our mortality, our greatest limitation. To determine to live the best life possible, and to promote the well-being of the Other given this awareness, is an outcome of the existential moment that brings epiphany. Csikszentmihalyi remarks that

> Aristotle believed that happiness was the result of the 'virtuous activity of the soul'. We agree with this aetiology to the extent that the proximal cause of happiness must also be a psychological state. External conditions like health, wealth, love or good fortune can help bring it about, but only if they are mediated by an appropriate subjective evaluation that labels the external conditions as conducive to happiness.
>
> *Csikszentmihalyi, 2014: 72*

Happiness is indeed the result of virtuous activity of the soul. But it cannot be only activity of the soul, as Csikszentmihalyi points out. Together, circumstance—environment natural, built, social—and soul activity engender moral agency conducive to human flourishing. The strength of the collective depends on the strength of individual persons; and it is true to say that the strength of a flourishing collective will affect the individuals of which it is composed. Martha Nussbaum, addressing the therapeutic role of philosophy in human flourishing, also argues that institutional context is important, and it was this, according to Martha Nussbaum, that Aristotle as well as the realised (Nussbaum, 2013: 505). She remarks that

> Hellenistic philosophers focus on improving the inner life of individuals, the objection goes, while neglecting the urgent task of constructing just political institutions. But any lasting improvement in human well-being requires institutional, and not just personal, remedies.
>
> *Nussbaum, 1999: 786*

Relatedly, in *Therapy of Desire* Martha Nussbaum writes of the Epicureans that for them,

> Politics is not simply, then, a matter of distributing the usual goods and offices. It involves the whole soul, its loves and fears and angers, its gender relations, its sexual desire, its attitudes to possessions, to children, to family. Epicureans see to what extent these allegedly "private" aspects of life have been warped by the traditions of an unjust and accumulative society; and they commend their personal therapy to us by asserting that individuals so warped can become good social agents in no other way.
>
> *Nussbaum, 2013: 504*

Unjust and accumulative societies are stunted collectives, of that we can be sure. Furthermore, the wholeness of the *cosmos* is inalienably tied into our human existence, as Carlo Rovelli pointed out for us, early in this book. Nussbaum also notes that the Stoics held that

> each of us is a citizen of the entire universe, a *kosmou politēs*. From its Greek beginnings, Stoic thought is anti-sectarian and anti-nationalist, turned firmly against the narrow loyalties that make politics focus on competition between groups rather than on rational deliberation about the good of the whole.
>
> *Nussbaum, 2013: 506*

For the Stoics, slavery, however, is never up for abolition because external circumstances do not count, as I pointed out, above: human dignity, the soul, is the premier interest. To demand the exercise of compassion is to run contrary to the ideals of Stoicism (Nussbaum, 2013: 506). It is clear to us today, that external circumstances do count, that hungry, ill, homeless, poor peoples, people ravaged by war and disease, often the making of fellow human beings who prosper from war and wealth and privilege have little or no economic resources. Yet they demand compassion and a recognition of the importance of these factors in all of our lives.

Nature, Beauty, and Art are each and all both immanent and transcendent aspects of collectives. Our exposure to them through culture cements our relationship with the collective and with each o/Other. But there is always more, the possibility of a 'view from above', a dislocation if you like of everyday perception. We always learn firstly from Nature. Love and disappointment, acceptance and rejection come to us, and we, to them. Human beings and culture as embodiments of Nature are our primary contact with the worlds we find ourselves in. We understand through our emotions, and our emotions create the possibility of knowing what is right and wrong. But our emotions are the basis rather than the product of moral life: rationality feeds apprehension of ourselves and o/Others as moral agents and recipients of moral action and outcomes. Perhaps we learn that we would not like others to feel as we feel when we are disappointed and rejected. After all, the emotions are the site of some of our most tender and uplifting as well as sad and confronting moments and memories. The expression of feeling through talking, through conversation, and the narrative in consequence that arises give us a language of morality. This is ethics, the habitual practice of being and becoming, of exploring emotional and rational states of being. And that is a basis of moral goodness in the human world: cruelty is the obverse, the basis of moral badness. This is where touch again enters the picture for morality is a product of how we *feel* when our environment affects us. Sight, sound, smell, taste, and touch itself both cause and influence how we feel and how to respond to those feelings.

Pierre Hadot remarks that '(f)or lived existential experience, the earth is nothing other than the immobile ground in relation to which I move, the fundamental referent of my existence' (Hadot, 2011: 253). We sense the immobile ground, we touch it. It touches us. Without touch we would have no contact with the ground. Lived experience *because of* touch is integral to all of our perceptions and conceptions of the world. This makes Nature, animate or inanimate, the ground of our being. Hadot also notes

> The "displacement of attention" of which Bergson speaks, as in the case of Merleau-Ponty's "phenomenological reduction," is in fact a conversion: a radical rupture with regard to the state of unconsciousness in which man normally lives. The utilitarian perception we have of the world, in everyday life, in fact hides the world qua world. Aesthetic and philosophical perceptions of the world are only possible by means of complete transformation of our relationship to the world: we have to perceive it *for itself* and no longer *for ourselves*.
>
> *Hadot, 2011: 254.*

Existential or epiphanic moments are moments in which attention is displaced; they are moments of conversion in which perception is transformed to the *for itself*. Moral *practice* converts us to the o/Other. We become good by being good, as Aristotle would have it. Yet a one-time experience of epiphany through a momentary glimpse of what it is to perceive no longer *for ourselves* can either motivate or make room for the moral imagination or enhance an already established moral disposition to act ethically. This is the case with Paul of Tarsus. When we are in states of unconsciousness, when action is always an automatic, unreflective response to so-called normality, we are, in all probability, operating in the *for ourselves* mode.

To come out of ourselves and see differently with a positive moral outcome is the essence of epiphany. This can happen *in spite of* the collective. The fact that it does happen augurs well for the collective if the collective can bear transformation and be prepared to abandon its *for ourself* mode of being.

So let us conceive of Jung's idea of a stunted collective as a collective that is habitually engrossed in its *for ourself* mode. Undoubtedly, the promotion of its own projects to the exclusion of consideration for the o/Other will reinforce the *for ourself.* Perhaps a collective can have an epiphanic moment, a moment when, existentially, it cannot bear to maintain the unconscious assumptions on which it has been operating. For what we take for granted, what is normalised for us all, is often a product of lack of reflection and of failure to acknowledge diversity, difference, rules made in the interests of those who are wealthy and powerful for example. The death of a great leader such as Gandhi might be such a moment. That is not to say that some would not be glad of his demise. That is not the point.

Rather, such a tragedy can turn on, at a collective level, the eye of reflection, of recognition that there are other ways of being. Transformation at a collective level is possible. That, indeed, is what figures like Gandhi, Mother Teresa, Nelson Mandela, or Eddie Mabo have taught us. Note, though, that the voice and action of the individual is pivotal here: members of collectives are the catalysts of change, so very often.[5]

And that is why Nature, Beauty, and Art are so central to morality: as foundation, as inspiration and trigger of imagination, as embodiment of human ideals. Surely, though, I am speaking of political action and change which is hardly relevant to either Beauty or Art? Part of the transformative power of Beauty and Art, indeed perhaps their main aspect, is their connection with both Nature and the human emotions; and the possibility of change. The Platonic ascent, to which Martha Nussbaum refers, revolves around an analysis of *eros* as depicted in Plato's *Symposium. Eros* and Beauty, *Eros* and Art, are intimately connected with touch. We are touched by both Beauty and Art, touched in such a way that we do feel differently, that we see differently as a result. We are inspired and our imaginations are fired. Without inspiration, we cannot flourish: inspiration and imagination assist the ascent of the Soul. Beauty is integral to both inspiration and imagination where these are positively transforming and stunted growth is addressed. Likewise, they assist the ascent of the collective soul, the intangible groupness of the whole group. Evidence of this intangible existence and operation lies in the politics practiced by any collective: community or group. Beauty both inspires and encourages the collective soul, as does Art.

If we are to take the idea of a flourishing collective, viz. the *whole* of what there is, cosmically, as one where stunted growth no longer is present, then these are fine examples of change and motivation that date back a very long time, to Hellenistic philosophy. Nussbaum also argues that from the perspective of political thinking, rules, laws, regulations are desiderata in the urge for the kind of social change that will enable goodness *as flourishing for the whole.* Inspiration and imagination are requisite demands of political change, and also of personal change. If one were to imagine a beautiful world in this *cosmos*, it is clear to see that anti-sectarian and anti-nationalist sentiments are contrary to any flourishing collective.

The best moments of many of our lives are those when we feel whole, accepted, and loved. In my view, these are moments when we are most embedded in Nature, for these are the gifts of Nature. And they come to us through Beauty and Art, so very often. I began this book with Annie Dillard. It seems, therefore, that I close with some more of her work.

In *Teaching A Stone to Talk*, she describes a time when she lived alone on a farm, a time she was overcome by the immensity of silence. Her description is too long to include here, but Dillard talks about being in the farm yard on a late summer morning in September when she was bashed 'broadside from the heavens above me', that there was 'only silence … the silence of matter caught in the act of embarrassment' something in the world's being 'unhinged', and of a woman's whistling such that 'the notes spread into the general air and became the weightier part of silence, silence's last straw'. She tells us that months later she was walking past the farm with a friend and that she announced that there were angels in the fields (where she had beheld silence). She says that '(o)nly their motion was clear (clockwise, if you insist); that, and their beauty unspeakable' (Dillard, 2017: A Field of Silence 137–143).

'Beauty unspeakable'. Nature. The written description of an artist. Transformation of Dillard and her readers. If it makes you feel good, you are more likely to practice good. That is morality, ethics.

Notes

1 Noted earlier in Chapter 3. See Nussbaum (2013) footnote 5, p. 15.
2 Hadot (2011). See Chapter 9, 'The View from Above' pp. 240 ff.
3 'Why not try/do x?' could be a catch question here. Or simply doing something that is different from, and represents, change.
4 As Martha Nussbaum points out, this is a problem reaching back to Hellenistic philosophies.
5 I am also aware that things can go belly-up, and that moments of revelation can lead to very undesirable moral outcomes. But the focus in these particular cases is not on enabling the collective as a whole to flourish, and thus to improve or remediate its stunted growth. Rather, the interests of a few, even a small collective are taken to be superior to the interests of the whole. Narrative based on lies is central in these cases: Hitler and the rise of Nazism and active anti-Semitism resulting in the holocaust is a good example of this as is the removal of Aung San Suu Kyi in Myanmar by the military junta and the current invasion of the Ukraine by Russia.

APPENDIX

Personal Experience

Experience 1

I was driving along the road by the river. I was aware that this drive is exceptionally beautiful with the gloss of the river, magnificent cloud and sky, the black swans, the hills and vineyards, the trees, the light and colour: oh, the light and colour! Simultaneously, I was aware that there was more than the beauty of the river and the wetlands, and the distant hills. I was listening to music, to a song I had known from long ago, a song I loved. There was an effect of the music, a kind of soundtrack that was accompanying me as I drove. I could not and did not speak; it was a moment of pure awareness. I was being transported by both Nature, and by Art. At some point, too, as language came back to me, I began to think about *The Acts of the Apostles*, Acts 5, and Ananias' and Sapphira's being struck down dead because they lied about profits from the sale of their property.[1] But this is a biblical story, a story from the Christian testament, and, somehow, I made a leap to Leonard Cohen's allusion to David of the Common Testament, to his singing, to please the Lord, 'Hallelujah'. Mystery and scripture, interpretation and ambiguity: the stuff of wonder, amazement and conundrum set in a mind, in a metal capsule zooming along a road. Music and moral lesson were running together as partners across the terrain of my mind which was simultaneously being flooded with some of the marvels of the natural world.[2] I was not only being transported, but enveloped by Nature, and by Art, simultaneously. For me, this became a moment of psychological transformation. This was an existential moment, epiphanic for the experience brought with it some deep changes.

Experience 2

> I was walking along a beach at Freycinet Peninsula in Tasmania on a morning late in winter. I came across an exquisite bi-valve shell, intact but without its small creature. Its colour was mauve/purple. In its wholeness, it was something I had not often seen. A short time later, I came across a woman who commented on the colour of the rocks (their redness) and who asked if I had been to the Bay of Fires, where the rocks are superior to even these specimens, so strong and enduring, studding the carmine shoreline. I told her that I had, and we agreed about their magnificence: 'You can't beat Nature' remarked the woman.

My experience depends on the possibility of this exchange between bodies and other, and it is an exchange, a reciprocal movement over which I can exercise only some control or even influence. What happened and why it happened is deeply bound up in notions of community and reciprocity. Individual as subject, and, what is equally the case, community as subject, are represented in not only mine, but any human experience. There is no move from individual subject as given and as the primary site of consciousness, to community as secondary, followed by a return; rather, there is an ebb and flow, I suggest, in what happened/happens and why. My experience, it seems to me, is not simply a result or effect of the interplay between individual and community: there seems to be something going on that is more than a cause and effect analysis can offer.

In the scene I described, I was clothed, I was driving a metal and plastic object with an engine powered by petrol, a carbon-based fuel, derived from ancient earth. There was so much more happening than word and sight. But it was an experience and a scene of reciprocity. Much of what was happening to, and around me, was fabricated through our human ability to transform Nature the natural environment and ecosphere, on the one hand, and to ignore and to it, on the other. Our ability to transform Nature is central to the symbolic practice of making of Art, and to Art's products. In a sense, as I drove along, I was a performance artist, taking part in a human production that is acted and re-enacted in nearly every human (and non-human at times) life on the planet in diverse forms on a daily basis. My doing what I was doing (driving, listening, watching), being what I was being (a human driver, inspired, a listener and watcher), following my own script, on a stage of human performance of the everyday, situated me as a creative actor in the natural world because I was able to imagine beyond the given, the before me. The trope of performance evokes the theatre, but allusions to performance here, is metaphorical. I might use metaphor to describe what was happening, but the being of my or anyone's life, is the very stuff of life.

Notes

1

> There was also a man called Ananias. He and his wife, Sapphira, agreed to sell a property;
>
> but with his wife's connivance he kept back part of the price and brought the rest and presented it to the apostles.
>
> Peter said, 'Ananias, how can Satan have so possessed you that you should lie to the Holy Spirit and keep back part of the price of the land?
>
> While you still owned the land, wasn't it yours to keep, and after you had sold it wasn't the money yours to do with as you liked? What put this scheme into your mind? You have been lying not to men, but to God'.
>
> When he heard this Ananias fell down dead. And a great fear came upon everyone present.
>
> The younger men got up, wrapped up the body, carried it out and buried it.
>
> About three hours later his wife came in, not knowing what had taken place.
>
> Peter challenged her, 'Tell me, was this the price you sold the land for?' 'Yes', she said, 'that was the price'.
>
> Peter then said, 'Why did you and your husband agree to put the Spirit of the Lord to the test? Listen! At the door are the footsteps of those who have buried your husband; they will carry you out, too'.
>
> Instantly she dropped dead at his feet. When the young men came in they found she was dead, and they carried her out and buried her by the side of her husband.
>
> And a great fear came upon the whole church and on all who heard it.

Given what I have written, we might wonder about the moral dimensions of this story. I have always found difficulty with this story: greed brings death and fear: but we might question motives here, and the absolutism of Peter, and his readiness to judge: 'would Jesus have acted as Peter did?' we might wonder when his message was love and compassion

2 Although I have found the relationship difficult to articulate, it is now not surprising that music and moral lessons accompanied each other in my mind. Obviously there was a biblical connection which brought the Acts of the Apostles together with the psalmist, David: the Common and the Christian Testaments together. But what is now more obvious to me is the conjunction of justice and beauty. The story of Ananias and Sapphira is not a beautiful story. It is a story about punishment for the betrayal of ideals and commitment, and then death. It is also a story that appeals to the vengeful God of the Common Testament rather than the loving God that Jesus proclaimed.

REFERENCES

Almond, P. C. (1982). *Mystical experience and religious doctrine: an investigation of the study of mysticism in world religions*. Berlin; New York; Boston: De Gruyter Mouton.

American Foundation for the Blind (2022). Helen Keller Biography https://www.afb.org/about-afb/history/helen-keller/biography-and-chronology/chronology

Aristotle, & McKeon, R. (1941). *The basic works of Aristotle*. New York: Random House.

Atamian, H. S., Creux, N. M., Brown, E. A., Garner, A. G., Blackman, B. K., & Harmer, S. L. (2016). Circadian Regulation of Sunflower Heliotropism, Floral Orientation, and Pollinator Visits. *Science*, *353*(6299), 587. doi:10.1126/science.aaf9793

Baird, J. (2020). *Phosphorescence: on awe, wonder and things that sustain you when the world goes dark*. Sydney: Fourth Estate.

Berent, I. (2020). *The blind storyteller: how we reason about human nature*. New York: Oxford University Press.

Berger, J. (1972). *Ways of seeing*. London: British Broadcasting Corporation; Harmondsworth: Penguin.

Bergstein, M. (2006). Freud's Moses of Michelangelo: Vasari, Photography, and Art Historical Practice. *The Art Bulletin*, *88*(1), 158–176. doi:10.1080/00043079.2006.10786283

Blackmore, S. J. (2005). *Consciousness: a very short introduction*. Oxford: Oxford University Press.

Bremer, R. (1976). Freud and Michelangelo's Moses. *American Imago*, *33*(1), 60. Retrieved from www.proquest.com/scholarly-journals/freud-michelangelos-moses/docview/1289742437/se-2?accountid=14723

Brentano, F., Kraus, O., & McAlister, L. L. (1995). *Psychology from an empirical standpoint*. London: Routledge.

Brison, S. J. (2002). *Aftermath: violence and the remaking of a self*. Princeton; London: Princeton University Press.

Brook, A, & Wuerth, J. (2020). Kant's View of the Mind and Consciousness of Self. In E. N. Zalta (Ed.), *The Stanford Encyclopedia of Philosophy*. Stanford: Metaphysics Research Lab, Stanford University.

Chalmers, D. J. (1995). Facing up to the Problem of Consciousness. *Journal of Consciousness Studies*, *2*, 200–219.

Chalmers, D. J. (1996). *The Conscious Mind: In Search of a Fundamental Theory*. Oxford, UK: Oxford University Press.

Chalmers, D. J. (2018). The Meta-Problem of Consciousness. *Journal of Consciousness Studies, 25*(9–10), 6–61.

Churchland, P. M. (2007). *Neurophilosophy at work*. Cambridge: Cambridge University Press.

Churchland, P. S., & Sejnowski, T. J. (2017). *The computational brain* (25th Anniversary edition). Cambridge, MA: MIT Press.

Colombetti, G. (2014). *The feeling body: affective science meets the enactive mind*. Cambridge, MA; London, England: MIT Press.

Csikszentmihalyi, M. (2009). *Flow: the psychology of optimal experience* (Nachdr. ed.). New York: Harper and Row.

Csikszentmihalyi, M. (2014). *Flow and the foundations of positive psychology the collected works of Mihaly Csikszentmihalyi* (1st ed. 2014.). Dordrecht: Springer Netherlands: Imprint: Springer.

Currie, G., & Ravenscroft, I. (2002). *Recreative minds*. Oxford: Clarendon.

Damasio, A. (2021). Feeling & knowing: Making minds conscious. *Cognitive Neuroscience, 12*(2), 65–66. doi:10.1080/17588928.2020.1846027

Damasio, A. R. (1994). *Descartes' error: emotion, reason and the human brain*. London: Penguin.

Damasio, A. R. (2000). *The feeling of what happens: body and emotion in the making of consciousness* (1st ed.). London: W. Heinemann.

Damasio, A. R. (2003). *Looking for Spinoza: joy, sorrow, and the feeling brain* (1st ed.). Orlando, FL: Harcourt.

Demarin, V., & Derke, F. (2020). *Mind and Brain*. Cham: Springer International Publishing.

Dennett, D. (1992). *Consciousness explained*. Coronado, CA: Bay Books.

Dickens, C. (1906). *Hard times*. London: Collins Clear-type Press.

Dillard, A. (1974 (2013)). *Pilgrim at Tinker Creek*. New York: HarperCollins.

Dillard, A. (2017). *Teaching a stone to talk: expeditions and encounters*. New York: Harper Perennial.

Eco, U. (2002). *Art and beauty in the Middle Ages*. New Haven; London: Yale University Press.

Eco, U. (Ed.). (2004). *On beauty*. London: Secker & Warburg.

Eniscuola. (2020). Loss of Biodiversity. Retrieved from www.eniscuola.net/en/argomento/biodiversity1/loss-of-biodiversity/causes-of-the-loss-of-biodiversity/

Frank, P. (2013). Carl G. Jung: The Artist Despite Himself. Retrieved from https://theredbookprints.com/in-the-news/carl-g-jung-the-artist-despite-himself/

Freud, S. (1914). The Moses of Michelangelo. In J. Strachey (Ed.), *Totem and taboo and other works* (Vol. XII), 209–238. London: Vintage Books The Hogarth Press. https://resolver.library.uq.edu.au/?&genre=article&sid=ProQ: atitle=Freud+and+Michelangelo%27s+Moses&title=American+Imago&issn=065860X&date=1976-04-01&volume=33&issue=1&spage=60 author=Bremer%2C+Rudy

Freud, S. (2001). *Totem and taboo and other works: 1913–1914* (J. Strachey, Trans. J. Strachey Ed.). London: Vintage.

Fukuoka, M. (2021). *The dragonfly will be the Messiah* (L. Korn, Trans.). London: Penguin Random House UK.

Gabriel, M., & Turner, C. (2017). *I am not a brain: philosophy of mind for the twenty-first century*. Cambridge, UK; Medford, MA: Polity Press.

Gallagher, S. (2017). *Enactivist interventions: rethinking the mind*. Oxford: Oxford University Press.

Gallagher, S., & Zahavi, D. (2021 Spring). Phenomenological Approaches to Self-Consciousness. In E. N. Zalta (Ed.), *The Stanford Encyclopedia of Philosophy*. Stanford: Metaphysics Research Lab, Stanford University.

Gaut, B., & Lopes, D. M. (2013). *The Routledge companion to aesthetics, third edition*. London and New York: Taylor and Francis.

Goff, P. (2017). *Consciousness and fundamental reality*. New York: Oxford University Press.

Goff, P. (2019). Science as we know it can't explain consciousness – but a revolution is coming. Retrieved from https://theconversation.com/science-as-we-know-it-cant-explain-consciousness-but-a-revolution-is-coming-126143

Grant, S. (2019). *Australia Day*. Sydney: HarperCollins Publishers.

Gray, F. (1990). *The subject/object distinction in mystical experiencing*. Canberra: Australian National University.

Gray, F. (2013). *Cartesian philosophy and the flesh: reflections on incarnation in analytical psychology*. Hove, NY: Routledge.

Gray, F. (2016). *Jung and Levinas: an ethics of mediation*. Hove, NY: Routledge.

Guan, F., Chen, J., Chen, O., Liu, L., & Zha, Y. (2019). Awe and Prosocial Tendency. *Current Psychology (New Brunswick, N.J.), 38*(4), 1033–1041. doi:10.1007/s12144-019-00244-7

Gyamtso, K. T. (1986/1988/1994). *Progressive stages of meditation on emptiness* (S. Hookham, Trans.). Oxford: Longchen Foundation.

Hadot, P. (1995). *Philosophy as a way of life* (M. Chase, Trans.). Malden, MA; Oxford, UK; Carlton, Australia: Blackwell Publishing.

Hadot, P. (1998). *The inner citadel: the meditations of Marcus Aurelius*. Cambridge, MA; London: Harvard University Press.

Hanson, R. (2009). *Buddha's brain: the practical neuroscience of happiness, love, & wisdom*. Oakland: New Harbinger Publications.

Heinämaa, S. (2007). Selfhood, Consciousness, and Embodiment: A Husserlian Approach. In *Consciousness. Studies in the history of philosophy of mind, 4*, 311–328. Dordrecht: Springer Netherlands.

Hepburn, R. W. (1966). Contemporary Aesthetics and the Neglect of Natural Beauty. In B. A. Williams & A. Montefiore (Eds.), *Analytical Philosophy*, 285–310. London: Routledge and Kegan Paul.

Hepworth, B. (1952). Barbara Hepworth: Carvings and Drawings, Section 4. Retrieved from www.tate.org.uk/art/artworks/hepworth-curved-form-trevalgan-t00353

Hildegard, S., & Fox, M. (1987). *Hildegard of Bingen's book of divine works with letters and songs*. Santa Fe, NM: Bear & Co.

Holroyd, C. (1903). *Michael Angelo Buonarroti with Translations of the Life of the Master by His Scholar, Ascanio Condivi, and Three Dialogues From the Portugese by Francisco d'Ollanda*. London: Duckworth and Company; New York: Charles Scribner Sons.

Hume, D. (1975). *A treatise of human nature: being an attempt to introduce the experimental method of reasoning into moral subjects: Book 1*. London: Fontana.

IPCC. (2021). AR6 Climate Change 2021: The Physical Science Basis. Retrieved from www.ipcc.ch/report/ar6/wg1/

Jacob, P. (2019 Winter). Intentionality. In E. N. Zalta (Ed.), *The Stanford Encyclopedia of Philosophy*. Stanford: Metaphysics Research Lab, Stanford University.

James, W. (1902). *The varieties of religious experience: a study in human nature*. New York: Longmans, Green & Co.

Jantzen, G. (1995). *Power, gender and Christian mysticism*. Cambridge: Cambridge University Press.

Jung, C. G. (1967). *Symbols of transformation* (H. Read, M. Fordham, & G. Adler, Trans. 2nd ed. Vol. 5): London: Routledge; Princeton: Princeton University Press.

Jung, C. G. (1971). *Psychological types* (R. F. C. Hull, Trans. Vol. 6): London: Routledge; Princeton: Princeton University Press.

Jung, C. G. (2009). *The red book = Liber novus*. New York: W.W. Norton & Company.

Kant, I. (1933). *Immanuel Kant's critique of pure reason* (N. K. Smith, Trans.). London: Macmillan.

Kant, I. (1998). *Critique of pure reason*. Cambridge: Cambridge University Press.

Kant, I. (2007). *Critique of judgement*. Oxford: Oxford University Press.

Kant, I. (2012). *Immanuel Kant: observations on the feeling of the beautiful and sublime and other writings*. Cambridge, UK: Cambridge University Press.

Kemal, S. A., & Gaskell, I. (Eds.). (1993). *Landscape, natural beauty and the arts*. Cambridge, UK; New York; Oakleigh: Cambridge University Press.

Kirk, R. (2021). Zombies. In E. N. Zalta (Ed.), *The Stanford Encyclopedia of Philosophy*. Stanford. Stanford: Metaphysics Research Lab, Stanford University.

Koch, C. (2012). *Consciousness: confessions of a romantic reductionist*. Cambridge, MA: MIT Press.

Koch, C. (2019). *The feeling of life itself: why consciousness is widespread but can't be computed*. Cambridge, MA: MIT Press.

Kounios, J., & Beeman, M. (2015). *The eureka factor creative insights and the brain*. London: Windmill Books.

Kristjansson, K. (2016). Awe: An Aristotelian Analysis of a Non-Aristotelian Virtuous Emotion. *Philosophia (Ramat Gan), 45*(1), 125–142. doi:10.1007/s11406-016-9741-8

Lang, A., Ott, P., Giudice, R. D., & Schabus, M. (2020). Memory Traces Formed in Utero – Newborns' Autonomic and Neuronal Responses to Prenatal Stimuli and the Maternal Voice. *Brain Sciences, 10*(11), 1–10. doi:10.3390/brainsci10110837

Levin, J. (Fall 2018). Functionalism. In E. N. Zalta (Ed.), *The Stanford Encyclopedia of Philosophy*. Stanford: Metaphysics Research Lab, Stanford University.

Lyons, N. (2019). *Signs in the dust: a theory of natural culture and cultural nature*. New York: Oxford University Press.

Macmillan, M., & Swales, P. (2003). Observations from the Refuse-Heap: Freud, Michelangelo's 'Moses', and Psychoanalysis. *American Imago, 60*(1), 41–104.

Maslow, A. H. (2012). *Religions, values, and peak-experiences*. Hawthorne, CA: BN Publishing.

McDonald, D. (2014). Joining the Diaspora of Deaf Memoirists: A Personal Account of Writing Deafness. *Am Ann Deaf, 159*(2), 77–86. doi:10.1353/aad.2014.0021

McGonagal, K. (2020). The joy of movement: how exercise helps us find happiness, hope, connection, and courage. Avery, NY: An Imprint of Penguin Random House.

Merleau-Ponty, M. (1995). *Phenomenology of perception*. London; New York: Routledge.

Metzinger, T. (2009). *The ego tunnel: the science of the mind and the myth of the self*. New York: Basic Books.

Mugeere, A. B., Atekyereza, P., Kirumira, E. K., & Hojer, S. (2015). Deaf Identities in a Multicultural Setting: The Ugandan Context. *African Journal of Disability, 4*(1), 1–e9. doi:10.4102/ajod.v4i1.69

Nagel, T. (2012). *Mind and cosmos*. Oxford: Oxford University Press USA–OSO.

Najarian, C. G. (2008). Deaf women: Educational Experiences and Self-Identity. *Disability & Society, 23*(2), 117–128. doi:10.1080/09687590701841141

Nehamas, A. (2001). A Promise of Happiness: The Place of Beauty in a World of Art. Retrieved from https://tannerlectures.utah.edu/lecture-library.php#n. https://tannerlectures.utah.edu/lecture-library.php#n

Noë, A. (2016). *Strange tools: art and human nature* (First paperback edition). New York: Hill and Wang, a division of Farrar, Straus and Giroux.

Nussbaum, M. (2001). *Upheavals of thought: the intelligence of emotions*. Cambridge; New York: Cambridge University Press.

Nussbaum, M. C. (1999). Précis of the Therapy of Desire. *Philosophy and Phenomenological Research, 59*(3), 785–786. doi:10.2307/2653797

Nussbaum, M. C. (2011). *Creating capabilities*. Cambridge, MA and London, UK: Belnap Press of Harvard University Press.

Nussbaum, M. C. (2013). *The therapy of desire: theory and practice in Hellenistic ethics* (With a New introduction by the author). Princeton: Princeton University Press.

Ohna, S. E. (2004). Deaf in My Own Way: Identity, Learning and Narratives. *Deafness & Education International, 6*(1), 20–38. doi:10.1002/dei.161

Oliver, M. (1992). *New and selected poems*. Boston: Beacon Press.

Pallasmaa, J. (2011). *The embodied image: imagination and imagery in architecture/Juhani Pallasmaa*. Chichester: John Wiley.

Pallasmaa, J. (2018). The Sensing and Knowing Body. In *The sentient archive*, 46–54. Middletown, CT: Wesleyan University Press.

Pappas, N. (2020 Fall). Plato's Aesthetics. In E. N. Zalta (Ed.), *The Stanford Encyclopedia of Philosophy*. Stanford: Metaphysics Research Lab, Stanford University.

Penfield, W. (2015). *Mystery of the mind: a critical study of consciousness and the human brain*. Princeton: Princeton University Press.

Penrose, R. (2016). *The emperor's new mind: concerning computers, minds and the laws of physics* (Revised impression as Oxford landmark science). Oxford: Oxford University Press.

Plato, & Cornford, F. M. (1970). *Theory of knowledge: The Theaetetus and the Sophist*. London: Routledge and Kegan Paul.

Plato. (1970). *The dialogues of Plato. Volume 2: the symposium and other dialogues* (B. Jowett, Trans. R. M. Hare & D. A. Russell Eds. [4th ed. revised]/edited by R. M. Hare & D. A. Russell; [reprinted]/with new introductions to the dialogues.). London: Sphere.

Plato. (1973). *Phaedrus and the seventh and eighth letters*. Harmondsworth: Penguin.

Plato. (1999). *The symposium*. London: Penguin.

Plato. (2003). *The Republic* (H. D. P. Lee, Trans. 2nd ed., Reissued with new Further reading). London; New York: Penguin Books.

Prinz, J. J. (2012). *Beyond human nature: how culture and experience shape our lives*. London; New York: Allen Lane, an imprint of Penguin Books.

Prinz, J. J. (2015). *The conscious brain: how attention engenders experience*. Oxford: Oxford University Press.

Reeve, C. D. C. (Summer 2016 Edition). Plato on Friendship and Eros. In E. N. Zalta (Ed.), *The Stanford Encyclopedia of Philosophy*. Stanford: Metaphysics Research Lab, Stanford University.

Rescorla, M. (2020). The Computational Theory of Mind. In E. N. Zalta (Ed.), *The Stanford Encyclopedia of Philosophy*. Stanford: Metaphysics Research Lab, Stanford University.

Rickless, S. (2020 Spring). Plato's Parmenides. In E. N. Zalta (Ed.), *The Stanford Encyclopedia of Philosophy*. Stanford: Metaphysics Research Lab, Stanford University.

Ricoeur, P. (1991). Narrative Identity. *Philosophy Today, 35*(1), 73.

Ricoeur, P. (2012). *Time and narrative* (K. McLaughlin & D. Pellauer, Trans. Vol. 1). Chicago: University of Chicago Press.

Rovelli, C. (2015). *Seven brief lessons on physics* (S. Carnell & E. Segre, Trans.). UK: Allen Lane: Penguin Random House.

Rudd, M., Vohs, K. D., & Aaker, J. (2012). Awe Expands People's Perception of Time, Alters Decision Making, and Enhances Well-Being. *Psychological Science, 23*(10), 1130–1136. doi:10.1177/0956797612438731

Russon, J. (2003). *Human experience philosophy, neurosis, and the elements of everyday life*. Albany: State University of New York Press.

Russon, J. (2017). *Sites of exposure: art, politics, and the nature of experience*. Bloomington, IN: Indiana University Press.

Särkämö, T., Tervaniemi, M., & Huotilainen, M. (2013). Music Perception and Cognition: Development, Neural Basis, and Rehabilitative Use of Music. *Wiley Interdisciplinary Reviews Cognitive Science*, *4*(4), 441–451. doi:10.1002/wcs.1237

Sartwell, C. (2017 Winter). Beauty. In E. N. Zalta (Ed.), *The Stanford Encyclopedia of Philosophy*. Stanford: Metaphysics Research Lab, Stanford University.

Schopenhauer, A. (1844). *The world as will and representation third book* (R. B. Haldane & J. Kemp, Trans.). In W. contributors (Ed.) (2nd ed.). Wikisource.

Schopenhauer, A. (2012). *World as will and idea (Vol. 3 of 3)*: Project Gutenberg. Retrieved from www.gutenberg.org/ebooks/40868

Senate Report on CIA Torture. (2014). Senate Report on CIA Torture. Retrieved from www.humanrightsfirst.org/senate-report-cia-torture

Siewert, C. (2017). Consciousness and Intentionality. In E. N. Zalta (Ed.), *The Stanford Encyclopedia of Philosophy* (Spring 2017 ed.). Stanford: Metaphysics Research Lab, Stanford University.

Smith, A. (1904). *An inquiry into the nature and causes of the wealth of nations* (Vol. 1, 2). Retrieved from http://oll.libertyfund.org/title/237

Sogyal, R. (1992). *The Tibetan book of living and dying* (P. Gaffney & A. Harvey Eds. Rev. and updated ed.). London: Rider.

Sparrow, T. (2014). *The end of phenomenology metaphysics and the new realism*. Edinburgh: Edinburgh University Press.

Sparrow, T. (2017). Ecological Trust: An Object-Oriented Perspective. *Philosophy Today (Celina), 61*(1), 99–115. doi:10.5840/philtoday2017320149

Spinoza, B. D., & Gutmann, J. (1949). *Ethics preceded by on the improvement of the understanding*. New York: Hafner.

Stoljar, D. (2020). Physicalism. In E. N. Zalta (Ed.), *The Stanford Encyclopedia of Philosophy*. Stanford: Metaphysics Research Lab, Stanford University.

Strawson, G. (2004). Against Narrativity. *Ratio*, *17*(4), 428–452. doi:10.1111/j.1467-9329.2004.00264.x

Suzuki, D. T. (1964). *An introduction to Zen Buddhism*. New York: Grove Press.

Taylor, J. B. (2009). *My stroke of insight*. London: Hodder.

Thompson, E. (2010). *Mind in life: biology, phenomenology, and the sciences of mind*. Cambridge, MA; London: Belknap.

Thompson, E. (2011). Living Ways of Sense Making (Structure of Behavior). *Philosophy Today*, *55*, 114–123.

Thompson, E., & Varela, F. J. (2001). Radical Embodiment: Neural Dynamics and Consciousness. *Trends in Cognitive Sciences*, *5*(10), 418–425. doi:https://doi.org/10.1016/S1364-6613(00)01750-2

van der Kolk, B. A. (2015). *The body keeps the score: mind, brain and body in the transformation of trauma*. London: Penguin Books.

Varela, F. J., Thompson, E., & Rosch, E. (2016). *The embodied mind: cognitive science and human experience* (revised edition). Cambridge, MA; London, England: MIT Press.

Wansbrough, H. (1985). *The New Jerusalem Bible: standard edition*. New York: Doubleday.

Wells, H. G. (1993). *The war of the worlds*. London; Rutland, VT: J.M. Dent; C.E. Tuttle.

WHO. (2020). Biodiversity. Retrieved from www.who.int/globalchange/ecosystems/biodiversity/en/

Zahavi, D. (2007). Self and Other: The Limits of Narrative Understanding. *Royal Institute of Philosophy Supplement*, *60*, 179–202.

Zahavi, D. (2008). *Subjectivity and selfhood: investigating the first-person perspective*. Cambridge, MA: MIT Press.

Zahavi, D. (2015). You, Me, and We The Sharing of Emotional Experiences. *Journal of Consciousness Studies*, *22*(1–2), 84–101.

Zahavi, D. (2016). The End of What? Phenomenology vs. Speculative Realism. *International Journal of Philosophical Studies*, *24*(3), 289–309. doi:10.1080/09672559.2016.1175101

Zahavi, D. (2018). Consciousness, Self-Consciousness, Selfhood: A Reply to some Critics. *Review of Philosophy and Psychology*, *9*(3), 703–718. doi:10.1007/s13164-018-0403-6

INDEX

Note: Endnotes are indicated by the page number followed by "n" and the note number e.g., 28n7 refers to note 28 on page 7.